SUPERVISION IN TEACHER EDUCATION LABORATORIES
A Series of Three Monographs

Inquiry into Teaching Behavior of
Supervisors in Teacher Education
Laboratories

Margaret Lindsey and Associates

A Theory of Supervision in Teacher
Education

Gilles Dussault

Preparation of Supervisors for Work
in Teacher Education Laboratories

Margaret Lindsey

Teachers College Press
Teachers College, Columbia University
New York, New York

INQUIRY INTO TEACHING BEHAVIOR OF SUPERVISORS

IN TEACHER EDUCATION LABORATORIES

Margaret Lindsey and Associates
Teachers College, Columbia University

Teachers College Press
Teachers College, Columbia University
New York, New York

LB
2153
.L5

AUTHORS

Richard Brown, Association for Supervision and Curriculum Development, Washington, D.C.

Father Edward Hancko, St. Paul's Mission Training College, Rhodesia

Ruth Heidelbach, Wheelock College, Boston

Miriam Hoffman, Hofstra University, Long Island

Theodora Kimsey, Towson State College, Maryland

Margaret Lindsey, Teachers College, Columbia University, New York

Arlene Low, Farmington State College, Maine

Norma Mertz, Eastern Michigan University, Ypsilanti

Floyd Waterman, University of Nebraska, Omaha

CONTRIBUTORS

Anna Beth Brown, Beaverton, Oregon

James Canfield, Teachers College Project in Afghanistan

Margaret Cobban, New Jersey State College, Glassboro

Jean Hill, University of Ontario, Canada

Dorothy Masters, Portland, Oregon

Robert Mullin, City University of New York--Queens College, New York

PREFACE

The central and integrating element in the professional education
of teachers is the professional practice itself, that is, teaching. Many
reasons can be advanced in support of this proposition. Not the least of
these is the potential of this focus for enlisting a student's personal
identification, early in his preparation, with a professional practice
and the consequent power of such identification as a motivating force.
Close association with teaching and teachers can cause a student to raise
important questions, to sense disequilibrium, to recognize need for
knowledge and skill, and to feel a growing commitment to excellence in
his chosen profession. His questions, his awareness, and his feelings
can be important ingredients in his motivation to pursue knowledge relevant
to his growing understanding of the professional practice. Encounter with
teachers and teaching, while he is engaged in study of teaching, can
increase his sensitivity to differentiation in style, verify his observation of dimensions of professional practice that are relatively common to
all, and contribute to his impatience to develop his own uniqueness as a
teacher. Adequately designed and conducted, study of teaching can have as
a major outcome the student's commitment to continuing scholarship in the
study of his own practice as a professional. Few outcomes would seem to
merit greater priority.

A professional program with study of teaching at its center necessitates laboratories where many and diverse opportunities are presented for examination of teaching and matters relevant to it. Laboratories may be simulated as well as real; they may be in schools, colleges/universities, or elsewhere. A student may engage in general observation of practice as well as close examination of his own and others' behavior; he may study both the art and the science of teaching and their interrelationship. Some laboratories may function primarily as centers for the discovery and verification of knowledge; others may be utilized chiefly for the dissemination of what is already known.

Today the use of laboratories by students of teaching is severely limited. It is not uncommon to find a professional program in which the student's exposure to laboratory-type study is confined to student teaching, and often this exposure is provided more to allow a student to demonstrate his teaching ability than to engage him in study of teaching. Current conceptions of professional laboratories, if they may be inferred from practice, are inadequate for programs that make study of teaching the organizing and integrating focus of professional preparation.

If students in education are to focus much of their study on teaching and if important parts of this study are to be carried on in laboratories, staffing these laboratories with competent professionals is essential. Guiding a young person in his development of a deep and meaningful concept of teaching, helping him to analyze the many facets of teaching, encouraging his expression in his own teaching behavior of what he is as a person, and providing him with sources and resources pertinent to his questions and to his efforts to understand and improve his teaching behavior--these are tasks that demand professional expertise.

As students' opportunities to study teaching in a laboratory setting have been limited in the past by prevailing concepts of student teaching as the central (and often the only) laboratory experience, so they have also been limited by reason of inadequate supervision in the laboratory. Neither the time nor the expertise has been available to cooperating or supervising teachers to enable them to perform their roles with excellence. It can be predicted with reasonable confidence that the matter of time will be resolved with greater partnership between colleges and schools in teacher education, with more attention to specialized career opportunities in teaching, and with growing awareness of the impact of laboratory experiences on students of teaching. Also, money can buy time, and greater financial resources will become available for this aspect of teacher education. Lack of expertise in working with students in professional laboratories is quite another matter, however. The fact is that too little is known about this expertise.

The series of three monographs, of which this is the first, is intended to contribute to knowledge about this expertise and how it may be acquired. The present monograph sets the stage through examination of the current and predicted nature of professional laboratory experiences in the education of teachers. It reports some exploratory studies of the teaching behavior of persons supervising in laboratories and concludes with a consideration of the status of knowledge with regard to supervisory behavior in professional laboratories. The second monograph presents a theoretical basis for determining what is known about the teaching behavior of supervisory personnel and the findings from application of a retroductive method in determining the status of knowledge in the field. It concludes with recommendations on the further development of a middle range theory of teaching by supervisors. Finally, the third monograph of the series advances proposals on the graduate specialized preparation of supervisors for work in teacher education laboratories.

Contributions to the series represent the work of a group of professional educators now located in different institutions of higher education but each of whom recently completed his doctoral dissertation at Teachers College, Columbia University and was sponsored by the editor of the series. Authors are identified with their contributions in each monograph.

The series is addressed to teacher educators in school and university settings who assume responsibility for the guidance of students in their study of teaching. It is hoped that the monographs will stimulate continued effort to bring to bear on problems of teaching in laboratories a scientific mode of investigation. Classroom teachers engaged in advanced graduate preparation for work as supervisors in professional laboratories should profit from giving consideration to the content. The publications should be useful to graduate professors who plan and conduct programs designed to assist their students in development of expertise as supervisors in professional laboratories.

Margaret Lindsey
September 1, 1969

TABLE OF CONTENTS

Chapter I

PROFESSIONAL LABORATORY EXPERIENCES IN

TEACHER EDUCATION--1970

Margaret Lindsey

The nature of professional laboratory experiences in teacher
education during the next decade is being determined in large measure by
conditions observable today. This chapter identifies a few of these conditions that have an integral and significant influence on professional
preparation of teachers and notes some of their implications. What will
be required, if the full potential of professional laboratory experiences
is to be achieved in teacher education, is then considered.

Some Determinants of the Nature and Scope of
Professional Laboratory Experiences

Contemporary developments, some resulting from availability of
new knowledge and others representing a return to formerly held notions
now understood more fully, make necessary a re-examination of the setting
that gives purpose and direction to professional laboratory experience in
the education of teachers. Modifications in purposes, programs, and
organization of educational institutions at all levels are clearly
discernable.

Reformulated Objectives of Schooling

Instructional objectives have a one-to-one relationship to definition of teacher roles and of the abilities required if those roles are to be performed with competence. Bloom and his associates presented a detailed analysis of objectives in the cognitive domain in 1956.[1] They classified intellectual skills and emphasized the importance of seeking to promote in pupils the higher levels of these skills--synthesis, application, and evaluation. In 1961 the Educational Policies Commission published its second statement on the purposes of American Education.

> The purpose which runs through and strengthens all other educational purposes--the common thread of education--is the development of the ability to think. This is the central purpose to which the school must be oriented if it is to accomplish either its traditional tasks or those newly accentuated by recent changes in the world. To say that it is central is not to say that it is the sole purpose or in all circumstances the most important purpose, but that it must be a pervasive concern in the work of the school. Many agencies contribute to achieving educational objectives, but this particular objective will not be generally attained unless the school focuses on it. In this context, therefore, the development of every student's rational powers must be recognized as centrally important.[2]

This statement was in concert with many other pronouncements and activities growing out of re-examination of the objectives of instruction. Contemporarily, renewed attention was being given to inductive

---

[1]Benjamin S. Bloom (ed.), Taxonomy of Educational Objectives: Handbook I--Cognitive Domain (New York: David McKay Company, Inc., 1956); and David R. Krathwohl et al., Taxonomy of Educational Objectives: Handbook II--Affective Domain (New York: David McKay Company, Inc., 1964).

[2]Educational Policies Commission, The Central Purpose of American Education (Washington, D.C.: National Education Association, 1961), p. 12. (The first statement was published by the Commission in 1938.)

methods; widespread activities were going forward on definition of the
several disciplines and their structure; psychologists were gaining
important new insights on the individual, personal nature of learning,
especially concept development; and the outcomes of schooling were being
subjected to critical examination.

Convergence of these and other developments resulted in a recasting
of instructional objectives characterized by movement away from what is to
be learned to an objective of learning how to learn; away from acquisition
of isolated facts to an objective of understanding the key concepts, the
organizing structure of a discipline, and gaining control over its methods
of inquiry; away from ability to memorize and recall to an objective of
acquiring attitudes, skills, and knowledge that enable rational approaches
to confrontations with personal, economic, social, and political problems.

A marked differentiation between stated objectives for levels of
education, frequently characteristic of the past, began to disappear.
The kinds of objectives indicated above are appropriate for every level
of education, from pre-school programs through graduate universities.
As enunciated by the Educational Policies Commission, it is these objectives that provide direction and continuity for instruction at all levels
and in all areas.

Implications of new instructional objectives for teacher education
programs are too many to be detailed here. However, an illustration may
serve to elucidate the meaning of new objectives for professional
laboratory experiences. The body of knowledge about teaching has key
concepts around which it can be organized; a definable group of key
questions provides direction for verification and discovery of knowledge

relevant to the field; and there are methods of inquiry, some general and others unique, particularly appropriate to the field. Hence, it can be argued that the central purpose of the student's participation in laboratory experience is to discover, to verify, and to test the meaning of key concepts about teaching and to do this by using those modes of inquiry appropriate to the field. If a student is to grasp the meaning of key concepts, he must work with those concepts; if he is to gain control over methods of inquiry, he must use those methods. In like manner, if he is to develop ability to take a rational approach to decision-making as a teacher, he must have opportunity to make decisions; he must practice a process of defining problems, collecting and analyzing pertinent data, hypothesizing consequences, testing hunches, and appraising results of his behavior. And, if he is to develop intellectual skills of synthesis, application, and evaluation, he must be required to use these skills. That a laboratory situation can and should provide the conditions that facilitate a student's having these kinds of experience is unquestionable.

Knowledge as a Basis for Decisions in Teacher Education

Education is taking on a new character as a field of study. One aspect of this new character is a persistent demand that decisions on program, instruction, and organization be based on verified knowledge. In teacher education the present demand for validated and verified knowledge arises in part from a lack of confidence in past decisions that rested on untested hunches or on uncritical transfer of propositions from one field to another.

Certainly scientific inquiry is not the only mode appropriate to analytical study of education. Yet, it is essential that education be studied in such ways as to produce valid and reliable predictions about cause-effect relationships. The difficulties and inadequacies of earlier studies and of the still unsolved problems in researching important questions are recognized. However, it is significant that variables assumed to be worthy of study are now being defined and described, and hunches about relationships among them are being subjected to empirical tests. As a result of such tests propositions are emerging which allow reasonable confidence in predictions based upon them.

A good deal of what is now done in the laboratory component of teacher education programs, including student teaching, is based on generalizations that are assumed to be valid. Little evidence is available to date on the validity and reliability of these assumptions. For example: it appears to be assumed that the amount of time a student spends in a laboratory (usually a classroom) has a direct positive relationship to the quality and quantity of his learning; that a teacher judged by his supervisors as an excellent classroom practitioner is therefore an excellent teacher educator in the role of supervisor of student teachers; that if a student shows ability to verbalize educational principles, he will therefore behave in terms of those principles while teaching in the classroom; that if a student is reasonably successful as a student teacher, he will therefore be successful on his own and without sustained guidance during his early years of teaching; that all students require the same time and experience in becoming competent beginning teachers. Such assumptions, and many others that could be identified, are now being examined with greater care, with more efficiency, and by more persons than

5

ever in the past. Evidence already accruing from these examinations suggests that many ideas, formerly held as unshakable, must be open to question.

As findings from current and future studies, testing assumptions and discovering new relationships relevant to provisions for laboratory experience, are verified and subjected to field examination, increased knowledge will be available for use in planning and conducting programs. Precisely what these findings will imply for specific practice remains to be seen. There are, however, some general and pervading implications of import in considering the future of professional laboratory experiences. Some of these are significant for the laboratory and the persons working in it.

Study of Teaching

Until quite recently there had been little direct study of teaching either by scholars in education or by students in training. Former investigations of teaching actually focused for the most part on teacher characteristics and teacher effectiveness. Only in limited ways did researchers examine teacher behavior. Of course, not all that needs to be learned about teaching can be found by direct focus on behavior of teachers while teaching. It is clear now, however, that teaching behavior can be defined and described, that such behavior can be studied in its own right, and that study of teaching behavior can yield significant findings.

A recent publication reviews some of the popular studies of teaching and, in connection with each review, proposals are presented on "Implications for Improved Teacher Education." A sampling of some of these implications will serve to illustrate the kinds of contribution studies of teaching can be expected to make to programs of professional laboratory experiences.

> . . . Smith's work could be used as an analytical instrument to assess the teaching behavior of preservice students. The preservice teacher could teach a single concept to a limited number of students. His instruction could then be followed by analysis of a tape to determine the degree of his success in teaching a concept. After the analysis, some reteaching could occur with appropriate corrective measures. . . . The analysis aspect of this work could occur in the usual methods courses or perhaps could find its way into a theory and laboratory course on teaching.[1]

> . . . Focusing, extending, and lifting within the three major cognitive processes are important functions for the teacher. Care should be taken when working with the prospective teachers in this area. They need sufficient time and practice and must experiment with formulating open-ended questions and developing appropriate sequences during their teacher preparation work.[2]

> . . . Theoretical analyses of teaching are as important as theories of learning and should be developed alongside learning theories rather than inferred from them.[3]

> . . . the system (Flanders) is an analytical tool for describing and analyzing the kinds of verbal interaction that take place between the teacher and his students. . . . and some attention should be given to its use for and in programs of teacher education.[4]

> Although he and his associates were concerned primarily with research rather than with prescription of practice, there are a variety of implications arising from Bellack's work because of the basic descriptive nature of the investigation. First of all, his system of analysis is highly developed and can therefore be used as an analytic tool by preservice students to ascertain the kinds of linguistic behavior occurring in a regular classroom or in some simulated or laboratory setting.[5]

---

[1]American Association of Colleges for Teacher Education, <u>Conceptual Models in Teacher Education</u>, ed. John R. Verduin, Jr. (Washington, D.C.: The Association, 1967), p. 14.

[2]<u>Ibid</u>., p. 25.   [3]<u>Ibid</u>., p. 31.   [4]<u>Ibid</u>., pp. 40-41.   [5]<u>Ibid</u>., p. 52.

Further comment on current research on teaching is unwarranted here. (Detailed consideration of this research appears in Chapter II.) The point to be understood here is that studies of teaching, as going forward now, provide new foci, new methods, and new tools that are already finding expression and use in the laboratories of teacher education. Although there appears to be need for caution against transferring research tools and methods to pedagogical purposes, it is nonetheless clear that both classroom and laboratory experiences of future teachers will be modified to take into account the growing body of knowledge about teaching behavior and the increasingly effective modes of collecting and analyzing data on teaching behavior.

Re-definition of Teacher Education

Current developments suggest a re-definition of certain notions about teacher education. Traditionally, the line between preservice and in-service teacher education has been arbitrary and distinct. For the most part, college and university personnel have assumed responsibility for preparation of a young person during his college years and have abruptly ceased concern for his welfare once he was placed in his first year of teaching. At this point, school personnel have taken over responsibility. The gap created between preservice preparation and first years of teaching has long been recognized as undesirable.

If, in addition to being liberally educated persons, teachers are to be scholars who are predisposed toward and capable of scientific inquiry into their work, four years of post-high school education are clearly not enough. But the answer is not to be found in merely increasing the number of years required in college prior to taking on responsible teaching assignments. What is called for is a continuous program in study of teaching, and related matters, from the time of decision to go into teaching as a career to the final years of practice. In this sense, "teacher education" is a process that continues as long as a person is engaged in professional practice.

When, in a teacher's development, it can be predicted with confidence that he is able to and will assume responsibility for his own continued professional growth, he should be granted tenure and awarded appropriate status. His environment should include a range of opportunities from which he can select those best suited to his interests and needs. Up until that time, however, he should be involved in a planned and systematic program of teacher education. In this sense, the term "preservice teacher education" becomes obsolete, and "teacher education" refers to preparation for teaching that extends from early in the collegiate years to the granting of tenure as a professional practitioner. "Pre-tenure teacher education" is thus more appropriate.[1]

Acceptance of the latter definition of teacher education has significant implications for programs of laboratory experiences. Such programs will have to be viewed as continuing through the early years of teaching. Marked distinctions now present between pre-student teaching experiences, student teaching, and internship teaching will need to be eradicated. The corps of persons who assume major responsibilities for

---

[1]This point of view has long been advocated. See, for example, National Education Association, National Commission on Teacher Education and Professional Standards, New Horizons for the Teaching Profession (Washington, D.C.: The Association, 1961).

the guidance of novices in the profession will have to be drawn from both schools and colleges. These persons will have to work as partners in the enterprise, partners whose work is equal in quality but different in kind. Regulatory measures affecting licensing of both novices and those who work with them will need to be devised. Specialized preparation will be required if college and school members of the corps of teacher educators are to function optimally. New arrangements to provide time and resources for concentrated study by students of teaching and by their teachers will be needed.

In addition to modifying the definition of teacher education so as to extend both upward and downward vertically, the contemporary scene makes clear a need to re-emphasize extension horizontally. The term "teacher education" is still employed by some to refer to the professional sequence, or to those parts of the total program generally conducted by schools and departments of education. Such use of the term is misleading, if not completely erroneous. For example, teaching strategies and tactics are integrally related to the nature of the discipline being dealt with. Hence study of a discipline by a prospective teacher should contribute not only to his control over the key principles and methods of that discipline but also to his developing concepts of teaching those principles and methods to the young. Objectives of general education encompass outcomes that are critical for future teachers, and without achieving those objectives a person can hardly be said to be ready to teach at any level of education. Specific study of teaching as the core of the professional sequence both profits from and contributes to study in general education and in specialized fields. Hence, the education of teachers is carried forward not alone in the professional component but in the other components as well.

Earlier reference was made to instructional objectives. It was suggested then that objectives being advanced as important at the lower levels of education are equally relevant at higher levels and in teacher education. One of the clear implications of these new instructional objectives in teacher education is a shift from programs to prepare technicians to programs designed to prepare professionals; a shift from emphasis on practice in use of techniques and devices to emphasis on intellectual activities of analyzing, diagnosing, hypothesizing, testing, searching, synthesizing, applying, evaluating--abilities essential to the fundamental task of decision making. This shift in emphasis is also part of an observable re-definition of teacher education. Implications of this shift for professional laboratory experiences are obvious.

The Teacher as Member of a Team

In ever so many ways, teachers of the future will be working as members of teams: teams of peers who plan and conduct programs for large groups of youngsters; teams of workers with differentiated functions and status who combine efforts to assist pupils in a single classroom; teams of various specialists who join in investigations and research. Implications of the increasing utilization of teams in schools are numerous and range widely in their potential impact. There are, however, some major implications for the future of professional laboratory experiences.

In one sense, traditional student teaching programs might have provided for students and their supervising teachers excellent

opportunities to develop the behaviors essential to team membership.
Team spirit and teamwork have always been necessary if these two persons
were to provide appropriate educational opportunity for pupils and for
each other. Although the importance of teamwork has always been recognized, almost no attention has been given to analysis of its properties
and to deliberate development of behaviors needed in team situations.
Review of the problems and difficulties in situations where various team
organizations have been employed in schools reveals that team members are
quite unprepared to assume roles they must assume, roles that are different from those demanded of the teacher who works alone with a group of
pupils in a self-contained classroom. Clearly professional laboratory
experiences should provide opportunity for all concerned to give needed
emphasis to team membership and teamwork, to identify more precisely
roles and functions, and to develop in specific terms competencies essential to productive teamwork.

Another way in which new concepts in staffing schools and classrooms will have direct influence on laboratory experiences is that
personnel in the laboratory situation will be multiple rather than single.
The scope and sequence of the future teacher's experience in this setting
will of necessity take on new and different dimensions. He may move
upward in a status hierarchy of team members, as he proceeds with his
teacher education. He may become a member of a peer team and gradually
develop the peer relationship. He may attach to specialized functions
or special curriculum areas for intensive study.

Laboratories are destined to have a range of personnel, beyond
classroom teachers, working in them. College professors and school-

12

attached people with specialized functions are likely to be active in the setting where the student engages in laboratory experience. Addition of such persons makes more complex the nature of the team and the diversity of activities taking place in the laboratory. The student will, in one way or another at different points in his preparation, be involved with these college professors and other specialists as team members. Indeed, some of his most important experiences will be had with teams of this nature.

Although major emphasis will continue to be focused on providing experiences that help a student progress toward confidence and competence as sole responsible agent in a self-contained classroom, programs of laboratory experiences will need to include plans for inducting the novice into this team setting and preparing him for making maximum contribution as a team member.

Technology and the Education of Teachers

Today there can be no question about the significance of technological developments for teacher education. Potential contributions of electronics to all parts of the program are still beyond imagination. In reality and in concrete ways, however, the availability of new electronic devices offers means for making vast changes and important improvements in programs of professional laboratory experiences.

One of the most important activities of the student and others in the professional laboratory is observing, recording, and analyzing behavior--pupil behavior, teacher behavior (their own and others'), and the interaction of teachers and pupils. Supervising teachers have long assumed responsibility for describing and analyzing student teachers' behavior; students at all levels of preparation have long been asked to observe, record, and analyze pupil and teacher behavior. It must be admitted that, while desirable outcomes were sought, very often the observing, recording, and analyzing of behavior by both students and teachers suffered tragically from inadequacy of focus, from lack of objectivity in recording, and from superficial techniques of analysis. But current developments in research are beginning to provide precise foci for both observing and analyzing behavior.[1] Electronics provide the means for recording, storing, and retrieving data.

Many experiences that formerly required a student's presence in the laboratory classroom can now be provided through the tube. Important stages in a student's discovering or testing his own ways of dealing with teaching situations, formerly almost exclusively a part of student teaching, can now be confronted in simulated settings, where the student's behavior can be electronically recorded, played back immediately for analysis, and where he can make immediate sequential attempts to test planned modifications in his behavior.

Some important questions need to be considered by those who plan programs of laboratory experiences, simply because electronic devices are available. What is it that students can best accomplish in simulated situations? What is the potential transfer of learning from simulated situations to real situations? What degree of emphasis should be put on

---

[1]For a comprehensive overview, see Anita Simon (ed.), Mirrors for Behavior (Philadelphia: Center for the Study of Teaching, Temple University, 1968).

detailed analytical approaches to analysis of behavior that has been recorded? To what extent should students in preparation be expected to master use of complex systems of analysis, systems developed primarily for research purposes? If it can be anticipated that students will gain considerable competence as teachers before undertaking what has been called in the past student teaching, what should be the nature of their experiences in the classroom with groups of pupils and when should these experiences occur in the program?

Another category of questions relates to the competence of those who work with students at the several levels of teacher education. Particularly important here are questions concerning the needed preparation of school personnel if they are to be able appropriately to use technology in working with students and beginning teachers.

Still another set of questions arises from consideration of the placement of equipment for use by students in teacher education. In this area it may be profitable for teacher educators to examine how those in medical education have dealt with these questions. Schools of medicine seldom establish separate laboratories in order to provide professional experience for students. They tend more to utilize the hospital setting, making provisions within it for special equipment and opportunities. It is doubtful that education can afford the setting up of laboratories in colleges and universities that duplicate laboratories that ought to be an integral part of every school. Even if each such duplication could be afforded, it is doubtful that it is wise.

It is difficult to separate the current research on teaching from the utilization of electronic devices, as both developments impinge upon programs of laboratory experiences. The former depends in important ways upon the latter; and the latter appears to be exploited more for research purposes than for instructional purposes. With the urgent demand for empirically tested knowledge, and all the forces in the educational setting in colleges and universities that put priority on research, there is high potential for unwise and indiscriminant use of both research and electronics in the pedagogical situation. Without question, there is substantial overlap in benefits that can be derived by students from their participation in activities designed to produce knowledge and those designed more specifically to assist students in the acquisition of knowledge and skills. Danger seems to lurk, however, in situations where researchers "use" students and programs to accomplish their own ends in knowledge production and do not give priority to teaching when such priority is essential to students' acquisition of knowledge.

Individualization in Teacher Education Programs

Ultimately what is hoped for as the outcome of a teacher education program is a person who finds satisfying self-expression in his individual, personal style of encounter with others in the teaching act. In his editorial in a special issue of the Saturday Review on "The New Computerized Age," Cousins comments:

> The essential problem of man in a computerized age remains
> the same as it has always been. That problem is not solely
> how to be more productive, more comfortable, more content,
> but how to be more sensitive, more sensible, more propor-
> tionate, more alive.
> . . . .
> The reason these matters are important in a computerized age
> is that there may be a tendency to mistake data for wisdom,

> just as there has always been a tendency to confuse logic
> with values, and intelligence with insight.[1]

Cousins is calling attention to the danger that lurks in an over-emphasis on or misuse of the miracles of an electronic age. For those responsible for professional laboratory experiences, the message needs to be taken quite seriously. Beware of focus on the scientific that loses sight of the humanistic in teaching. Look out for strategies and tactics that may suffocate the individual. Guard against neglecting the fundamental import of values and wisdom in efforts to support logic and to base all operations on factual data.

If a student is to be valued for what he is and can become, his individual, personal style will need to be nurtured deliberately by those who work closely with him over a period of time. As Combs[2] and others have suggested, there are definable ways of nurturing the person in the student, of protecting and encouraging his individuality.

Problems associated with providing for individualization in laboratory experiences are numerous. Partially they are inherent in the course-credit-class syndrome that dominates higher education. Some are rooted in the bigness, the mass production, and the general depersonalization in many colleges. Others result from interpretation of degree and certification requirements. Whatever the problems, arising from whatever sources, and whatever their magnitude, ways must be found to provide more

---

[1]Norman Cousins, "The Computer and the Poet," _Saturday Review_, July 23, 1966, p. 42.

[2]Arthur Combs, _The Professional Education of Teachers_ (Boston, Mass.: Allyn and Bacon, 1965).

adequate opportunity than is now available for each individual to progress
at his own rate and style in becoming a teacher.

It is possible to conceive of the laboratory as a place where
people, things, and ideas are present and where activities of many sorts
are in progress. Planned sequences of various kinds of experience would
be readily available, and each student would be guided carefully in
progression from one level to another. Some students would quite quickly
initiate experimental projects with groups of pupils; others might not
take such initiative until much later. Some would engage over a considerable period of time in dyadic and small group situations, while
others proceeded to work with groups of class size. Some would begin
systematic analysis of their own behavior almost immediately; others
might postpone this activity until a later time. Some would begin to
test their own ideas about the organization of content for instruction,
while others were still quite dependent in this respect. And some would
make great leaps, thus bypassing planned interim experiences. In such a
setting, the range of activities would encompass both the cognitive and
the affective, both the normative and the personal, individual dimensions
of teaching.

Reference to personal style brings to mind the significance of the
art of teaching. While witnessing the volume of research and experimentation now in process on the science of teaching, it is sobering to note
that inquiries into the art of teaching, into personal styles of teaching
behavior, into the affective dimensions of a teaching-learning environment
are conspicuous by their negligible number. Witness the training programs
for student teachers that focus on their scientific analysis of their

teaching behavior. But note the relatively rare existence of similar programs that focus on sensitivity, perception, and feeling. For a long time, literature on student teaching and other laboratory experiences has paid homage to the principle of individual differences and admonished teacher educators to take this principle into account more adequately. The admonition has had too little effect.

Only a few of the determinants that might have been selected for consideration have been identified here. Certainly many others might have been selected. For example: current, delayed attention to specialized educational opportunities for the disadvantaged child (whether located in an urban, suburban, or rural area; whether the disadvantage is rooted in social, ethnic, racial, or economic conditions) clearly dictates modifications in professional programs to prepare teachers for schools populated by such pupils. Contracts being developed between teacher groups and boards of education, contracts that set limits on teacher activities and use of time, create conditions heretofore not encountered in making arrangements between schools and colleges for laboratory experiences. Disappearance of the single-purpose institution and the consequent placement of teacher education in competition with other programs in larger, multipurpose institutions, while resulting in major advantages for students in teacher education, sometimes make more difficult and complex the task of planning and conducting adequate programs of laboratory experiences.

Laboratories in Teacher Education

It is difficult to imagine a program to prepare professional practitioners without laboratories where the professional practice can be studied and experienced by the student. It is not surprising, therefore, that laboratories of all kinds are emerging.

Educational Laboratories

There are demonstration laboratories, experimental laboratories, learning laboratories, research and development laboratories, educational laboratories. There are laboratories in schools; others in colleges and universities. There are laboratories removed from direct association with either schools or universities. There are local, state, regional, and proposed national laboratories. And there is a persisting, though slight, emphasis on the schools as laboratories in which research and experimentation should flourish.

Note the differences in laboratories suggested by the following:

In discussing "the definition and reallocation of school and university roles in training teachers" Shaplin states:

> Clearly the colleges and universities are best fitted to provide the teaching, the libraries, the laboratories, and the climate of thought in which mature minds can develop. The university is best prepared to undertake basic inquiry, to formulate and design research studies aimed at answering fundamental questions in education though the studies may be carried out in the schools.[1]

Wiles, presenting his ideas about "The Teachers We Need," says:

---

[1]Judson Shaplin, "Practice in Teaching," Teacher Education: A Reappraisal, Elmer Smith, editor (Urbana, Illinois: Phi Delta Kappa, 1966), p. 20. (Italics not in original.)

We need to develop ways for building the college of education program around laboratories devoted to the investigation of the school program--laboratories in which the
teaching staff of the college conduct or participate in
research activities which will increase their understanding and give them greater assurance for making statements
about teaching, learning, and the school program. The
laboratories must also provide experiences for students
so that they will see themselves as investigators in the
process of education.[1]

Psychiatrist Kubie suggests:

This is precisely what we need in education: research
schools to parallel research hospitals. The best schools
of tomorrow will be the schools which carry on daily
basic research in every detail of the education process,
schools with observation chambers and recording equipment,
schools with research staffs, schools with at least as
many professionals as students. There must be research
scientists in education working beside the general practitioners of education, just as there are research scientists
in medicine working beside the practitioners, each learning
from the other.[2]

Reporting on "A Model of a Cooperative Resource Demonstration Center"

Corrigan says:

The Center will provide a resource for university and
city school personnel to meet for pre-service and
in-service education programs, and through its television
network and other communication avenues, bring the
resources of the Center to and from other city schools,
local industry, museums and libraries, and the University.

It will also offer opportunity for researchers, graduate
students and University faculty members to participate
with city school personnel in some of the significant
research that needs to be undertaken for improving urban
education. It is hoped that this Center will serve as a

---

[1]Kimball Wiles, "The Teachers We Need," Journal of Teacher
Education, 17:262-268, Summer, 1966. (Italics not in original.)

[2]Lawrence S. Kubie, "Research in Protecting Preconscious Functions
in Education," paper presented. Mimeographed. (Italics not in original.)

model system, as part of a program to help a large city attack the problems of urban education.[1]

Shaplin speaks of laboratories in the university, where basic inquiry is carried on. He suggests that some studies may use the schools, but these will be formulated and designed by university personnel. In this sense, the school may be a source of data and school personnel may become subjects in studies. It can reasonably be assumed here that Shaplin is referring to the production of knowledge relevant to educational questions.

Although Wiles is not explicit on details, it appears that he is talking about regular schools as laboratories where both college teachers and students might be active. Kubie, on the other hand, seems clearly to be talking about specialized schools, set apart from others because they are centers for scientific inquiry. Relationship of these selected research centers to other schools and to universities can be inferred from relationships that usually prevail between research hospitals, other hospitals, and schools of medicine.

In Corrigan's plan it is explicitly stated that some research will be carried on by university professors, but it is also made clear that pre- and in-service teachers might work side by side with other school and university personnel, and in addition, other specialists from the community.

These four and many other types of research laboratories will be

---

[1] American Association of Colleges for Teacher Education, Committee on Studies, Subcommittee on School-College Relationships in Teacher Education, Cooperative Structures in School-College Relationships for Teacher Education, Brooks Smith and Patrick J. Johnson, editors (Washington, D.C.: The Association, 1965), p. 91.

needed in advancing knowledge in education. Experience of three and
four decades ago, however, should serve to caution against certain
dangers. For example, sharp distinctions between the production of
knowledge through basic scientific inquiry in university laboratories and
production of knowledge through scientific inquiry in practical settings
(schools) would seem to be unwise. Similarly, previous experience does
not augur well for sharp distinctions between selected research-experi-
mental schools and regular schools. Earlier distinctions of these kinds
surely contributed to the slow pace of dissemination and utilization of
research findings; to unfruitful relationships between behavioral scientists
and educators; to unproductive relationships between schools and colleges.
Furthermore, such distinctions did not help young people preparing to
teach to acquire the notion that teachers had responsibility for continuous inquiry into their work; rather, they may have contributed to
students' feeling that all responsibility for advancing knowledge about
problems and practices in education belonged to university professors.
Too often this feeling was accompanied by disdain for research and theory
on the part of practitioners and by equal disdain for practical considerations on the part of researchers and theorists.

The School as Laboratory

A good many teacher educators, as well as supervisory and administrative personnel in schools, believe that classroom teachers should be
able to carry on some research activities. A few educators have gone so
far as to suggest that fundamental research in education in the future
will be done in classrooms and schools and will be done by school personnel,

particularly teachers. No one would seriously propose that all the needed research could or would be done by practitioners or in classrooms. But there are persuasive reasons why much research will be designed and carried out by teachers and their colleagues in school settings. First, if present proposed programs in which preservice students get experience in analytical study of their teaching, in participating in research projects of various sorts, in having specialized preparation in research methodologies, and in learning by appropriate methods of inquiry are even in some measure effective, we may reasonably expect that as classroom teachers they will sustain their interest and their desire to continue to take an investigatory approach to their problems. Second, if schools and school systems continue the trend toward locally sponsored and conducted research, teachers will continue to be involved in such research. Third, some investigations carried on by university personnel will of necessity involve teachers and pupils in studies of various sorts. Fourth, if standards for admission to full standing in the profession of teaching continue to rise and conditions surrounding teaching continue to improve, more able students will enter teaching, and these persons will require opportunity for continued inquiry as a condition for teaching. Conditions that encourage scholarly behavior--time, space, resources, rewards--will need to be available to all teachers.

Schools are slowly but surely becoming centers of inquiry. Behavioral scientists, subject matter specialists, professors in colleges and universities, practitioners at all levels in the schools, and research specialists now join forces in constructive investigations related to school programs, pupil personnel, school organization, teaching, and learning. This range of specialists and the studies they conduct are beginning to be, and will increasingly be, part of the setting in which students have professional laboratory experiences.

More and more scholars in the behavioral and social sciences, aware of the disadvantages of their earlier isolation from reality in the schools, are turning their interest and attention to conducting studies in the schools. A few of these scholars have already made outstanding contributions by applying their disciplined approach to study of educational problems. And, in the future it can be expected such scientists while conducting their studies in the school as the laboratory will involve students and teachers in these studies. These same persons will be the college teachers of future teachers in their so-called foundation courses.

Increased numbers of scholars in subject matter fields have developed interest in and concern for the teaching of their specialties in elementary and secondary schools. Some such persons have begun to devote their scholarship to investigation of teaching and learning, of scope and sequence in program, and of materials of instruction in the schools. And these are the same persons who are the college teachers of future teachers in their specialized teaching fields; these, too, are now a part of the laboratory into which the prospective teacher goes for important kinds of experience.

Professors of education, who too often in the past became more removed from reality of the classroom with each year of service in a teacher education program, are now in greater numbers moving into the schools as laboratories for their own continuing scholarly study. Here too, students in preparation for teaching encounter the same professionals in the college classroom and in the laboratory center.

When the school is seen as a center for inquiry, not only for pupils but for teachers and teacher educators as well, and when college and school personnel are closely related in the conduct of investigations, it would seem very likely that remarkable changes would occur in the total professional education of future teachers. For one thing, college teachers who are themselves involved in school programs may share their involvement with their students, may actually have their students participate with them, thus making the laboratory a far more important part of the total professional sequence than it has been heretofore. For another, school personnel who are involved with college teachers and with college students may discover new professional stimulation and reward as they take on their roles as scholarly teacher educators. Also, it is reasonable to predict that both the substance and the processes of programs designed to prepare teachers will gradually modify toward emphasis on learning how to learn about education, schools, pupils, teaching, materials, and learning, and that the processes employed will be modes of inquiry appropriate to study of educational problems. In other words, it is reasonable to predict that much of what is now didactic teaching in college classrooms will in the future be guidance of students in schools and school classrooms as laboratories.

Supervision in the Professional Laboratory

Programs to prepare professional practitioners require laboratories in which the novice may experience the practice. That assumption calls forth little dissent. It has been basic in the designing of professional education programs from their beginning and it continues to support emphasis on student teaching and other kinds of laboratory experiences in teacher education today. An assumption that such laboratories might be of diverse types, in addition to schools and classrooms, is not as widely accepted. Current practice, in contrast to theory, opinion, and admonition, would suggest that professional laboratories are seen more as practice and testing centers than as centers where students and their supervisors are engaged in continuous study of teaching.

If a student's work in a professional laboratory is to contribute to his preparation as a scholar teacher—to cause him to develop a rewarding personal style of teaching, to help him gain control over modes of inquiry appropriate to continued study of his behavior, to assist him in discovering, verifying, and systematizing knowledge related to practice— then a laboratory must be a place where he does more than copy and perfect someone else's practice and where his supervisors are primarily concerned with more than assessing his level of competence by predetermined, sterile, unimaginative, and often unvalidated standards of teaching performance.

What is of great importance in the professional laboratory is the quality of experience students have in it. And, this quality is determined, in very large measure, by those who provide the guidance of students in the laboratory. Regardless of where they come from—schools, colleges or universities, outside agencies—and regardless of their specialties—academic discipline, curriculum, teaching, psychology, and so on—persons who work with students in a professional laboratory take on unique roles that require special expertise.

Persons who guide students in laboratories are traditionally referred to as supervisors. Conventional practice of such persons has tended to place undue weight on the overseeing, managing, directing, and assessing functions and too little emphasis on the guiding, supporting, stimulating, and facilitating functions. Supervisors need to and do perform a range of functions in a teacher education laboratory. However, in a laboratory where students are engaged in study of practice and in examination and improvement of their own behavior, it is logical to assume that the supervisor's primary function is teaching. If this is so, and we believe it is, then supervisors' teaching behavior may be subjected to systematic study just as any other teaching behavior can be studied.

It has been argued here that professional laboratory experiences are taking an increasingly important place in the education of teachers, that diverse types of laboratories are required, that the central purpose of laboratory experiences is study of teaching, and that the quality of a student's experience depends greatly upon the supervision provided in the laboratory. Although supervisors perform varied functions, their central function in a professional laboratory is teaching. Supervisory teaching can be studied systematically and eventually knowledge can be accumulated that will enable predicting relationships between supervisory behavior and student learning in the laboratory. The studies reported in this monograph are beginning steps toward describing supervisory behavior by means of systematic study.

Chapter II

THE STUDY OF TEACHING IN THE TEACHER EDUCATION LABORATORY
Margaret Lindsey and Ruth Heidelbach

A laboratory for teacher education is a place where students
endeavor to learn, each in ways appropriate for him, as much as possible
about the art and science of teaching. Many and varied activities are
carried on there by persons who differ in interest, ability, experience,
status, and function. Despite the variation in focus and character of
specific enterprises, a common goal is shared by those who work in the
laboratory. That goal is to increase knowledge about and ability in the
practice of teaching.

In such a laboratory, an advanced scholar may be researching by
use of sophisticated methods a well defined problem in his specialty. A
professional teacher may be collecting and analyzing data relevant to an
hypothesis about alternate approaches to involving pupils in independent
inquiry. A psychologist may be recording and analyzing language patterns
of pupils from contrasting backgrounds. A media specialist may be conducting a controlled experiment on the use of a multi-sensory program in
science for young children. Pupils are key persons in this laboratory,
whether it be located in a university or in a school, whether it be

simulated or real.

A teacher education laboratory, in addition to housing the kinds of activities and persons indicated above, is a place where the young are being inducted into the profession. These are the students of teaching who will tomorrow be providing leadership in schools. What they become, how they feel, what they know, what they can do will be significantly influenced by their experiences in the teacher education laboratory. A great deal of what happens to them will be the result of their own interpretations of values and behavior they observe in those around them—veterans in the profession. But what they observe, how they interpret, what activities they engage in and how these activities are examined are the responsibilities of the mature professionals who work with them in the laboratory.

The induction process ideally begins very early in a student's collegiate career and extends through the first few years of teaching. Because the process is intimate and individual, the sequence, pacing, and nature of activities in the laboratory, and in other parts of the preparatory program as well, will vary from one inductee to another. Each prospective teacher will have differentiated kinds of experience in assuming responsibility for teaching. According to his needs and his readiness, he will tutor one child, or teach a small group, or function as the teacher with a class of pupils; he will work independently or in close association with professionals and non-professionals in a classroom where he has specific tasks to perform. He will practice a specific teaching behavior under conditions that permit him to retrieve a record of his behavior and to analyze it as a basis for repeated practice. He will engage in these and other such activities with the close guidance of designated personnel in the laboratory. The profit accruing to him, and eventually to pupils whom he will teach in the years ahead, will depend largely on the expertness of those who help him to examine and intellectualize his experience.

In teacher education parlance, the designated persons responsible for guiding the novice in the laboratory are usually referred to as supervisors. Although they may have other responsibilities (e.g., classroom teachers teach pupils and discharge other obligations of professional members in a school complex; university teachers teach students and similarly meet other obligations as members of the scholarly community), a primary function performed by them is the guidance of one or more prospective teachers in the laboratory. In the discharge of this function, the supervisor creates the conditions that promise to help each student progress successfully from where he is to what he may reasonably be expected to become as a teacher and helps him to make maximum use of the conditions. He functions in this regard precisely as any teacher functions. In every sense, the supervisor in the laboratory is a teacher and his central activity as a teacher educator is teaching the future teacher about teaching.

Knowledge about the conditions in a teacher education laboratory that can be predicted to be effective and how such conditions may be established is very inadequate. A similar statement might be made about teaching in any setting. However, recent years have seen a resurgence of interest in and study of teaching in elementary and secondary classrooms, and the results are encouraging. While the momentum in study of teaching has gathered and more and more scholars have devoted their energies to production of research in this area, very little attention has been given to special kinds of teaching in non-classroom settings. Almost no attention has been focused on teaching by supervisors in the teacher education laboratory.

The fact that too little is known about supervision in the teacher education laboratory places obligation on those with interest in and responsibility for work there to produce some systematic studies that may increase what is known and contribute to improvement of supervisory practice. Since the primary function assumed by laboratory supervisors has the central attributes of teaching, it is reasonable to assume that the current wave of studies of teaching might be a productive source for suggestions on approaches to examination of supervisory behavior. The present chapter reports briefly on selected studies of teaching and considers implications of them for systematic study of supervision in the teacher education laboratory.

Studies of Teaching: Examples

Few persons in education are unaware of the basic rationale prompting the present intense effort to study teaching in its own right, as contrasted with inferring knowledge about teaching from study of learning or limiting study to personality and general methods. Professional educators have been admonished to turn their attention directly to examination of teacher behavior. Gage asserted that "to explain and control the teaching act requires a science and technology of teaching in its own right."[1] Taba advised "we must study teaching as it occurs in the class-room. . . ."[2] The admonishment has been taken seriously by a large number of scholars and the fruits of their efforts are important.

It is now clear that teaching is an exceedingly complex matter, that teachers confront a multiplicity of variables in each moment of their work, and that each situation has its own character and dimensions that must be taken into account. It is also clear that much preliminary research is required before predictive hypotheses about relationships between teacher behavior and learning outcomes can be tested.

Specific teaching behaviors must be described; valid and reliable means for collecting and analyzing data on those behaviors must be developed. Similarly with pupil outcomes: specific behaviors must be described and ways of collecting and analyzing data on those behaviors must be established. Only when such means are available for treating data on behavior variables can research efforts proceed to inquire into relationships between variables.

Contemporary investigators recognize the importance of descriptive studies as prelude to studies designed to test relationships and even-tually to advance predictive hypotheses. These investigators have developed and tested instruments for objectively recording and analyzing

---

[1]N. L. Gage, "Theories of Teaching," Theories of Learning and Instruction, Sixty-third Yearbook of the National Society for the Study of Education, Part I (Chicago: The University of Chicago Press, 1964), p. 273.

[2]Hilda Taba, Samuel Levine, and Freeman F. Elzey, Thinking in Elementary School Children, U.S. Office of Education Cooperative Research Project, No. 1574 (San Francisco: San Francisco State College, 1964), p. 44.

interaction in the classroom. They have produced classificatory systems for describing the interaction. Current studies of classroom interaction are rich in potential suggestions on how supervisory teaching behavior might be more systematically studied. A selected few of these studies are reviewed here.

Aschner and Gallagher viewed teaching as primarily linguistic in character. Linguistic meanings are communicated in classroom discourse and are related to the levels of thinking produced as teacher and learner deal with subject matter. Using an *a priori* category system adapted from Guilford's model of the intellect, these investigators analyzed records of secondary school classroom discourse, and classified teacher and learner interaction as related to thought processes by pupils.

Five major categories, each with sub-classifications of behavior, were developed.

I. Routine--includes routine classroom procedural matters such as management of the classroom, the structuring of class discussion and approval or disapproval of the idea or person. (Sub-categories: Management, Structuring, Verdict)

II. Cognitive-memory--the simple reproduction of facts, formulas and other items of remembered content through use of such processes as recognition, rote memory and selective recall. (Sub-categories: Recapitulation, Clarification, Factual)

III. Convergent Thinking--thought operation involving the analysis and integration of given or remembered data. It leads to one expected result because of the tightly structured framework which limits it. (Sub-categories: Translation, Association, Explanation, Conclusion)

IV. Evaluative Thinking--deals with matters of value rather than matters of fact and is characterized by verbal per- formance by its judgmental character. (Sub-categories: Unstructured, Structured, Qualification)

V. _Divergent Thinking_--individuals are free to generate
their own data within a data-poor situation, often taking
a new direction or perspective. (Sub-categories: Elabora-
tion, Divergent Association, Implication, Synthesis)[1]

Bellack and his associates described teaching in the classroom as

a language game.

Teaching is similar to most games in at least two respects.
First, it is a form of social activity in which the players
(teachers and pupils) fill different but complementary roles.
Furthermore, teaching is governed by the actions or moves
made by participants.[2]

These investigators examined classroom interaction to determine "the

functions these verbal actions served in classroom discourse and hence

the meanings that are communicated."[3] Examination of the data resulted

in the formulation of four major categories into which verbal action of

students and teachers could be classified. These were labeled pedagogical

moves.

Structuring--serves the pedagogical function of setting the
context for subsequent behavior.

Soliciting--elicits a response.

Responding--bears a reciprocal relationship to soliciting
moves and occurs only in relation to them.

Reacting--occasioned by a structuring, soliciting, responding, or prior reacting move, serves to modify and/or to rate
what has been said previously.[4]

---

[1]As reported in Anita Simon and E. Gil Boyer, _Mirrors for Behavior_
(Philadelphia: Research for Better Schools, Inc., 1967).

[2]Arno A. Bellack et al., _The Language of the Classroom_ (New York:
Teachers College Press, Teachers College, Columbia University, 1966),
p. 4.

[3]_Ibid._   [4]_Ibid._, p. 5.

The identification of these moves as basic units enabled the investigators to analyze verbal behavior of both teachers and students and to study the recurrent patterning in classroom discourse. It was found that pedagogical moves occurred in specific relation to each other, and these patterns of relationship were called teaching cycles. By using teaching cycles, the researchers concluded that it is possible to study the sequence of pedagogical moves and stylistic differences in terms of various dimensions of classroom discourse such as rate, source, and pattern, and that entire class sessions may be plotted showing movement from one kind of patterning to another.

Bellack and his associates were also "interested in the dimension of meaning represented by the content of the messages communicated. Analysis of classroom discourse revealed four functionally different types of meanings: . . ."[1] These four types of meanings became additional categories for the analysis of classroom discourse. They are:

II.   Substantive Meanings--refer to the subject matter of the class.

III. Substantive-Logical Meanings--refer to the logical processes involved with dealing with subject matter.

IV.   Instructional Meanings--involve such matters as assignments, materials, and routine procedures.

V.   Instructional-Logical Meanings--refer to didactic verbal responses.[2]

Flanders developed a system for recording and describing the climate of elementary classrooms and for determining the sequence of teaching behavior. Perhaps the most widely used of the many systems available,

---

[1]Ibid.   [2]Ibid., pp. 5-6.

this one is relatively simple but effective. Teacher Talk and Student Talk are the two large divisions of the system. Within Teacher Talk are categories of Indirect Influence and Direct Influence. Sub-categories under Indirect Influence are: Accepts Feelings, Praises or Encourages, Accepts or Uses Ideas of Children, and Asks Questions. Sub-classifications under Direct Influence are: Lecturing, Giving Directions, Criticizing or Justifying Authority. Student Talk is sub-classified by Response or Initiation. A category referred to as Silence or Confusion is included. A matrix for recording interaction by observers provides the framework for gathering information about the sequence of teacher and student talk.

In one of the earliest studies, Hughes defined teaching as "interaction with a child or group." She went on to say:

> The teacher has power, in contrast to the students, to arrange the learning environment, to decide the content to which attention is to be given, the standards that are to be maintained, and who is to do what.[1]

Within this conceptual framework trained observers recorded elementary classroom discourse and verbatim records of teaching were collected. One outcome of the analysis of the data was a system for describing the major functions teachers performed in the classroom, as follows:

- I. Control--Structuring, Regulating, Informing, Setting Standards, Judging.

- II. Facilitating--Checking, Demonstrating, Clarifying.

- III. Developing Content--Serving as Resource Person, Stimulating, Clarifying Content, Evaluating, Turning Questions Back to Class.

---

[1] Marie M. Hughes, "Utah Study of the Assessment of Teaching," Theory and Research in Teaching (New York: Bureau of Publications, Teachers College, Columbia University, 1963), p. 28.

IV. Personal Response--Meeting Requests, Clarifying
     Problems, Interpreting.

 V. Positive Affectivity

VI. Negative Affectivity[1]

Smith and his associates viewed teaching as a social phenomenon.

> Teaching is assumed . . . to be a social phenomenon,
> fundamentally the same from one culture to another and
> from one time to another in the same culture. It is a
> social action with its own distinctive elements, forms,
> regularities, and problems and takes place under what
> seems to be a relatively constant set of conditions--
> time limits, authority figures, student ability limits,
> institutional structures, etc.[2]

These investigators tape recorded verbal teaching behavior in secondary

classrooms and analyzed their data to define logical operations, i.e.,

"the forms verbal behavior takes as the teacher shapes the subject matter

in the course of instruction."[3] Categories resulting from the analysis of

the data were: Defining, Describing, Designating, Stating, Reporting,

Substituting, Evaluating, Opining, Classifying, Comparing and Contrasting,

Conditional and Inferring, Explaining, Directing and Managing Classroom.

In a series of studies following the report on the logic of teaching,

Smith and his associates extended their analyses of verbal interaction in

the classroom. Examination of larger units of discourse (larger than the

episodes used in the first study) in relation to specified objectives

---

[1]As reported in Anita Simon and E. Gil Boyer, *Mirrors for Behavior*
(Philadelphia: Research for Better Schools, Inc., 1967).

[2]B. Othanel Smith and Milton Meux *et al.*, *A Study of the Logic of
Teaching* (Urbana: College of Education, University of Illinois, Bureau
of Educational Research, 1963), pp. 2-3.

[3]*Ibid.*, p. 3.

resulted in a system of categories for describing teaching strategies as causal, conceptual, evaluative, informative, procedural, reason, rule, or system ventures.[1]

Taba and her associates defined teaching as ". . . an organic complex in which each individual act, such as an affective response or content structuring, acquires a different meaning depending upon the nature of the whole teaching-learning situation."[2] Using knowledge about the nature of thinking and the development of cognitive skills, these researchers constructed a set of categories, as follows:

I. Designation

    Child Gives   Child Seeks
    Teacher Gives   Teacher Seeks

II. Function
                            Management

    Agreement   Approval
    Disagreement   Disapproval
    Management   Reiteration
                            Direction
    Focusing   Extending Thought
    Change of Focus   Refocusing
    Controlling Thought   Deviating

III. Level of Thought

    Grouping and Labeling
    Interpreting Information
    Making Inferences
    Predicting Consequences[3]

---

[1] B. Othanel Smith et al., A Study of the Strategies of Teaching (Urbana, Illinois: Bureau of Educational Research, College of Education, University of Illinois, 1967).

[2] Hilda Taba et al., Thinking in Elementary School Children, U.S. Office of Education Cooperative Research Project, No. 1574 (San Francisco: San Francisco State College, 1964), p. 43.

[3] Ibid., pp. 199-207.

Much earlier Withall had suggested that the social-emotional climate in the classroom was a function of teacher behavior and related to
the conditions for learning on the part of pupils. He created a system
for classifying teacher statements along a continuum from "learner
centeredness" to "teacher centeredness." Transcripts of teacher behavior
were analyzed, using these categories: Learner Supportive, Acceptant or
Clarifying, Problem-structuring, Neutral, Directive, Reproving, Dis-
approving or Disparaging, and Teacher-Supportive.[1]

In 1967 Simon and Boyer edited an anthology which includes the
systems reported here and twenty additional ones.[2] Their work is a
valuable resource for those interested in study of teaching. It provides
not only clear presentations of the systems of categories, but also data
on the development and use of each system. A bibliography of approximately four hundred references is included. As Simon and Boyer indicate,
systems have thus far been constructed primarily for research purposes; a
few have been employed in teacher education programs, especially to help
student teachers or interns record and evaluate their own and others'
teaching behavior.

Implications of Current Research on Teaching for Study of
Supervision in Professional Laboratories

Although only a limited number of systems have been used with

[1]John Withall, "The Development of a Technique for the Measure-
ment of Social-Emotional Climate in Classrooms," Journal of Experimental
Education, 17:347-361, March, 1949.

[2]Anita Simon and E. Gil Boyer, Mirrors for Behavior (Philadelphia:
Research for Better Schools, Inc., 1967).

students-in-training, a good number of supervisors appear to have considerable confidence in them as one means for helping their students study their own teaching behavior. These same supervisors seem to be quite unaware of their own interaction in teaching future teachers; they seldom apply to their own teaching behavior the kinds of analysis they and their students apply to students' teaching behavior. Yet, there are persuasive reasons why supervisors in a teacher education laboratory should be studying their own behavior. As suggested earlier, the novice in the laboratory is making observations of the behavior of veterans and drawing conclusions about what it means to be a professional. It is to be hoped that the novice sees his supervisors as professional scholars, unceasingly searching for understanding and improvement of their own behavior. In addition, what the student-in-training focuses on, the kind of searching he does, the activities he engages in, the quality of his examination of what he does and of what goes on around him--these are highly influential in his development and they are the responsibility of his supervisors.

The idea being advanced here is that present studies of classroom teaching behavior are a source from which to cull concrete suggestions on how the teaching function of supervisors might be more systematically studied and consequently improved. Would it be profitable to focus study of supervision on the same or similar aspects of behavior as those studied in teaching? Might the methods and instruments developed in contemporary analytical study of teaching behavior be adaptable to similar study of supervisory behavior? Is it possible to study the logic of supervision, the language of supervision, and the substance of supervision as these have been studied in teaching? What is more important, might the growing body of knowledge about teaching, coupled with the increased significance of laboratory experiences in teacher education programs, stimulate professional educators toward conducting more rigorous study of precisely what goes on in such laboratories? Might the excitement of systematic study lead supervisors to innovative approaches in analysis of their own teaching behavior?

Specific supervisory teaching is usually individualized teaching; the student and the supervisor relate to one another as teacher and learner in a dyadic situation. This one-to-one encounter is commonly referred to as a supervisory conference. Sometimes, however, the conference changes its dyadic mode and involves more than two individuals, as when, for example, a team of supervisors comes together with students in various patterns. There may be a conference with a cooperating teacher, student, and school supervisor, or a conference with a college supervisor, student, and cooperating teacher. Frequently college and/or school personnel perform some of their supervisory functions with a number of students in a seminar experience.

The objectives and content considered by individuals and groups in these settings may be derived from reality in the classroom, school, or other formal educational setting; or, they may be derived from laboratories where simulation and other similar techniques for study of teaching are being employed. Whatever the objectives and content being dealt with, the teaching by the supervisor can be subjected to systematic study to describe the interaction between him and his student(s), to examine the level of thinking his behavior elicits from the student, to note patterns and stylistic features, and so on. Similarly, the emotional-social climate

of the supervisory teaching situation can be studied, just as the classroom can be studied for the same conditions.

In addition to suggesting foci for study, current research on teaching has implications for the use and development of instruments and methods
for systematic study of supervisory behavior. Investigators might select
as a target a particular supervisory setting and test the feasibility of
existing instrumentation and methodology or postulate adaptations that seem
fruitful for study.

Instruments used in current research on teaching have been developed
to describe and analyze verbal and non-verbal aspects of teaching behavior.
Aschner, Flanders, Taba and Withall developed category systems by adapting
existing theoretical constructs from studies of intellectual and/or cognitive development, studies of thinking, or studies related to emotional
and social phenomena. Application of previously developed constructs to
the analysis of new data has been described as an _a priori_ method. Bellack,
Hughes, and Smith analyzed data on teaching behavior by using an _a
posteriori_ method. They derived classificatory systems from the data.

Supervisory teaching might be studied by means of either approach.
Certain of the many systems of categories already available should be
tested to discover what information their application to supervisory teaching would yield. Theories in related fields[1] should be examined to determine their potential use in development of principles and categories that

-----

[1]The second monograph in the present series examines the Rogerian
Theory of Counseling and from that basis, proposes a structure for developing a theory of supervision in the teacher education laboratory. Written
by Gilles Dussault, this monograph will be available within four months
after the date of publication of the present one.

might be employed in analysis of teaching by supervisors.

Laboratory teaching may have some unique features, especially because it is often tutorial in setting. Unless some studies of supervisory teaching proceed on an a posteriori basis, it will be impossible to know whether it is unique, and if it is, in what ways. Furthermore, it will be difficult, if not impossible, to establish the validity of available systems for use in describing supervisory teaching. As has been emphasized earlier, being able to describe with accuracy and objectivity the teaching behavior of the supervisor is prerequisite to research on effectiveness of that behavior.

The basic method used in much of the research on classroom teaching is some form of content analysis. Content to be analyzed is obtained by trained observers or by mechanical recording of teacher behavior. There is no reason to believe that this basic method would not be profitable in the study of teaching by supervisors in a teacher education laboratory. Data collection is relatively simple because of new media and technology. Video recordings, readily available at present, provide more precise records of both verbal and non-verbal behavior. Wireless recordings make possible collection of data without dependence on place and setting.

Smith sets forth a definition of a possible logic of teaching.

By "logical operations," which are the focus of our study,
we mean the forms which verbal behavior takes as the
teacher shapes the subject matter in the course of instruction. For example, the teacher reduces concepts to linguistic patterns called definitions; he fills in gaps between
the student's experience and some new phenomena by facts
and generalizations related in a verbal pattern referred
to as an explanation; he rates objects, events, etc., by

reference to facts and criteria related in a pattern
called evaluation.[1]

By adapting Smith's definition of logical operations to possible supervisory discourse, certain key elements of his definition can be considered.
These elements are: (1) forms of verbal behavior, (2) shaping subject
matter, and (3) course of instruction. Logic of supervisory discourse
then might deal with "forms" of supervisory verbal behavior, "shaping" of
subject matter in interaction with a supervisee, and the "course" of
supervisory teaching.

Forms   may be defined as supervisory teaching patterns made
         up of a number of teaching operations.

Shaping may be defined as supervisory teaching strategies made
         up of a number of teaching patterns.

Course   may be defined as a larger scheme of supervisory
         teaching related to what it is the supervisor intends
         to teach. One might consider "course" or "scheme" as
         a curricular design. In this case, scheme deals with
         the structuring of facts, concepts, principles and
         generalizations about teaching.

Smith argues that teaching operations exhibit a structure that can
be observed and described. If supervisory teaching can be shown to have
sequences of behavior that contain patterns and strategies that are clearly
related to intended schemes, the logic of such teaching can be described.
One task of future investigators will be to determine the elements of
supervisory teaching, to hypothesize relationships among those elements,
and then to confirm or reject their hunches. Questions such as these will
be of concern to future researchers.

---

[1]B. Othanel Smith and Milton Meux et al., A Study of the Logic of
Teaching (Urbana: College of Education, University of Illinois, Bureau
of Educational Research, 1963), p. 3.

Although the methods and instrumentation that have been developed in study of classroom teaching are exceedingly useful as beginning points for research into the behavior of laboratory supervisors, it would be unfortunate if the imagination and scholarship of teacher educators were to be limited by what has already been done. It is to be expected that new approaches, new methodologies, and new instruments will emerge as supervisory teaching is subjected to rigorous study.

EXPLORATORY STUDIES OF SUPERVISORY

TEACHING BEHAVIOR

Chapters III-VII

Introduction

The studies reported in the next five chapters are initial explorations in the direction of systematic inquiry into supervisory teaching behavior. Their limitations are many, some intended and others the result of many kinds of inadequacies. Intentionally, they are confined to study of verbal behavior; they deal only with supervision of student teachers, and, furthermore, are limited to conferences that take place between the persons usually involved in student teaching programs. Systems of categories for describing the linguistic discourse in supervisory conferences that have been developed in the studies are crude beginnings. They have not been validated nor subjected to repeated study. Nevertheless, considerable importance can be attached to them because they are initiatory, and beginnings must be made. It is expected that future studies will be more advanced because these explorations have been presented.

Chapter III reports a pair of studies with common purpose and design but utilizing different bases for analysis. As early attempts to make some progress in the study of supervisory behavior, these researchers attempted the large task of describing supervisory behavior in conferences with student teachers and determining the impact of that behavior on the subsequent teaching by students. Important findings came from this effort. For example, it was found that supervisory behavior could be subjected to systematic study and analysis, and description of that behavior could be profitable to practicing supervisors. Students involved as subjects in this pair of studies responded with enthusiasm to the experience of having complete and objective data on their teaching as the substance of talk with their supervisors. Equally important, however, was the recognition of need for more and better schemes for describing the behavior of supervisors as a prelude to studies of the effects of that behavior.

The second study (Chapter IV) represents a totally different approach to the problem. Assuming a high degree of commonality between the way a counselor interacts with his client and the work of the supervisor with individuals, these researchers set out to do a content analysis of literature in both fields. Their intent was to test that assumption and, if it were found to be reasonably valid, they would then proceed to construct a model of categories that might become the basis for study of supervision as carried on when one individual confers with another about the problems of concern to one or both participants. The search and analysis of literature in counseling was fruitful and the model was constructed.

Chapter V reports a study in which protocol of eighteen conferences between cooperating teachers and student teachers were content analyzed. Here the purpose was to derive a set of categories from the data (a posteriori), a tedious and difficult kind of undertaking. The model that resulted should have considerable usefulness in that it represents the nature and substance of the conferring between a group of six classroom teachers and the students assigned to them. Replication of this method in attempts to build a system for describing and analyzing this important encounter in teacher education programs would appear to be very helpful.

A similar approach was used by the investigator who reports in Chapter VI. Here protocol of conferences between the college supervisor and cooperating teachers are analyzed and a model for describing the discourse in this critical team situation is derived. College supervisors who want to examine their verbal behavior as they work with cooperating teachers should find this study useful, not only because of the system of categories it presents, but also because the method is appropriate to individual and perhaps less formal study by any supervisor.

In Chapter VII a different teaching function of supervisors is examined and a different approach is made in the investigation. Two studies are reported. In one, a college supervisor examines teaching as performed in a seminar with prospective teachers. In contrast with other studies reported, this one was designed to involve students in a natural history method of observing their own teaching behavior in classrooms. In the other, a nurse educator analyzes the verbal interaction that took place in twenty-eight clinical conferences in each of which from eight to ten students participated. Combined, these studies begin to look at ways seminar teaching might be studied.

Chapter III

ANALYSIS OF TEACHING BEHAVIOR AS THE SUBSTANCE OF
CONFERENCES WITH STUDENT TEACHERS[1]
Arlene Low and Floyd Waterman

The two parallel studies described here were the first of a series focused on examination of the teaching behavior of those who work with students in professional laboratory experiences. Pioneer efforts in their field, they demonstrated forcefully the need for further study of supervisory behavior as college and school personnel work with students in teacher education.

Two studies, focusing on the supervisory conference and employing the same design and procedures, were carried out by two three-man teams. One study used selected principles of learning as evaluative criteria in analyzing records of student teachers' verbal teaching behavior. The other used pedagogical moves (Bellack) and a system of categories of cognitive processes as the basis for examination of the behavior.

---

[1]The two team studies reported in this chapter were conducted by Anna Beth Brown (Midwest Teacher Education Project, Chicago), James Canfield (Teachers College, Columbia University Project in Afghanistan), Margaret Cobban (New Jersey State College at Glassboro), Arlene Low (State College at Farmington, Maine), Robert Mullin (Queens College of the City University, New York City), and Floyd Waterman (Omaha University, Nebraska).

The purpose of each study was to discover whether there is a relationship between supervisor-student teacher conferences employing a planned, systematic approach to analysis of student teachers' behavior and subsequent teaching behavior of the student teachers.

The conference methods constituted the independent or experimental variables, and the classroom verbal teaching behavior of the student teacher the central dependent variable.

A Pair of Studies with Common Design and Procedures

Each of six college supervisors collected data on the verbal teaching behavior of three student teachers, and contributed data in the form of tape recordings of his conferences with those individuals. Data collected by all the members of a team were pooled for analysis. The design of each study included: (1) recording teaching sessions of student teachers; (2) analyzing, using a specific method of analysis, typescripts made from the tapes; (3) developing commitments for changed behavior by student teachers in supervisory conferences; and (4) inspecting typescripts of subsequent teaching sessions to identify evidences of implementation of commitments.

Recording and Retrieving Teaching
Behavior by Students and Supervisors

Five teaching sessions were recorded for each student teacher. Use of two microphones, one a lavaliere model, ensured verbatim records of the student teachers' verbal teaching behavior. Children's talk was usually, though not always, adequately recorded also. The subjects taught were those that emphasize conceptualizing: arithmetic, reading, language, science and social studies. The subject for each teaching session, its length, and the procedure to be used were decided by the student teacher and his cooperating teacher.

Typescripts were prepared from the tapes, and copies given both the student teacher and his college supervisor. Thus each had an exact record of the student teacher's talk in the teaching session. Each analyzed the record independently, using the agreed-upon system of analysis.

After analysis of the record, the student teacher and the college supervisor met to confer about the teaching. These conferences were also recorded. One topic considered in each conference was discussion of these analyses. Conference discussion was not, however, limited to this topic, but dealt with topics that either participant wished to discuss. Each conference included or concluded with the making of a commitment(s) by the student for changed behavior during subsequent teaching in an elementary school classroom.

Focusing on Commitments to Change Behavior

While each conference ranged widely and included consideration of various topics, it was expected that each should include one or more specific plans for changed behavior of the student teacher. In the conferences, these plans were referred to as "Next Steps," or commitments, and were usually written, as reminders for use in later planning. The following definition and criteria were used in identification of commitments.

Definition:

A commitment is a statement of intent to act in future teaching.

<u>Criteria</u>:

    A. A commitment may be stated by a student teacher or by a college supervisor.

    B. If the commitment is stated by the college supervisor, it must:

        1. have evolved from discussion in a conference,

        2. be supported by evidence that the student teacher accepted the projected action.

Because records of subsequent teaching sessions were examined for evidence of implementation of commitments made in conferences, commitments were the key to the studies. Conferences were planned. Both immediate needs of the student teachers and specific plans for future action were discussed in conferences. Appearance of such action in subsequent teaching sessions was taken as indication of the existence of a relationship between the conference and subsequent teaching behavior.

Selecting and Training Subjects

Students enrolled in the Preservice Program were carefully selected graduates of liberal arts colleges. Their individually guided graduate programs in professional education consisted of both course work and related direct experiences. Within one academic year and one summer, students acquired the understandings and skills necessary for beginning teaching.

Students admitted to the Program were eligible to take part in this investigation, but only those who indicated their willingness to participate formed the population pool from which the eighteen subjects were finally chosen. Those who were selected were representative of a cross section of the Program.

Before data collection began, a series of orientation sessions prepared both the student teachers and the investigators with skills necessary for the study. Training given the student teachers consisted of an introduction to educational research, to the importance of verbal teaching behavior, to the cycle of plan, teach, confer with the supervisor, plan again, teach again, and to use of the system of analysis to be employed by the respective research team.

Training of Investigators

While the investigators had received training in coding typescripts during their development of the study design, training continued through the orientation period, as the supervisors prepared materials for use of the student teachers, independently analyzed records of verbal teaching behavior, and compared their analyses with those of others. In the end, a high degree of agreement was reached among the members of each team.

Because supervisory conferences were so important a part of the study, and because the design rested on the supervisors' ability to assist student teachers to develop commitments during supervisory conferences, training in conferring techniques seemed essential. The supervisors developed a statement of assumptions concerning conferences and a list of guidelines.

The assumptions made were these: (1) A conference between a college supervisor and a student teacher is a particular form of a teaching-learning situation. (2) Supervisors' conference styles are and should be characteristic of the individual. (3) The major purpose of the conference is to help the student teacher grow, as a teacher and as a member of the teaching profession.

The following statement of guidelines was accepted by the investigators:

A. Both participants should prepare a plan for discussion prior to the conference.

B. The supervisor should try to establish an atmosphere of mutual trust and understanding. He should

   1. listen to and draw out the opinions of the student teacher.

   2. show respect for the student teacher's ideas.

   3. focus discussion on the teaching situation rather than on the person.

   4. give attention to the positive as well as the negative aspects of instruction.

C. The supervisor should help the student teacher identify specific areas of concern.

D. The supervisor should help the student teacher select that teaching behavior which he will attempt to change.

E. The supervisor and the student teacher should discuss specific ways of implementing these desired changes in behavior.

F. The student teacher should leave the conference confident of his basic potential as a teacher.

G. The focus of the conference should be on helping the student teacher to:

   1. identify, with some exactness, gaps between his aspirations and his actual behavior.

   2. diagnose his teaching to discover the reasons for the gaps.

   3. search for better behaviors that give promise of improvement.

   4. plan ways of putting these presumably better actions into practice.

5. consider ways and means of evaluating the effects
   of the presumably better actions.

A simple form with the two headings, Notes for Conferences and
Next Steps, was employed to facilitate planning conferences and recording
commitments. Both conference participants used the same form.

Up to this point the two studies were alike. The differences
between them were the means of analysis which formed the basis for supervisory conferences. One study used principles of learning as a means of
analyzing records of teaching. The other used pedagogical moves (Bellack)
and a system of categories describing cognitive processes.

Selected Learning Principles as the Basis for Analysis of Teaching Behavior[1]

There is no lack of precedent for studying and using principles of
learning in teaching. From the earliest days of the study of psychology
attempts have been made to help teachers translate findings about learning into guides for action in their teaching. Most professional programs
include courses in educational psychology. Few young teachers, however,
seem to be particularly successful in translating the findings of
psychology into teaching behavior. It was reasoned that direct, practical
guidance in doing this, during student teaching, might increase their
ability to base their teaching behavior on learning theory.

---

[1]James K. Canfield, Arlene F. Low, and Robert E. Mullin, "A
Principles of Learning Approach to Analysis of Student Teachers' Verbal
Teaching Behavior" (unpublished Ed.D. project report, Teachers College,
Columbia University, New York, 1965), p. 116.
    Hereafter in this chapter references to this study will not be
footnoted.

Definitions and Hypothesis to Be Tested

The term, principles of learning, as it is used in textbooks on teaching, refers to generalizations or concepts of different degrees of complexity and varying levels of abstraction. If guidance in the use of theory were to be practical, the statements of theory must be as simple and specific as they could be made. Since these statements differed in form and content from other statements having the same label, it was found necessary to define the term as it was being used in the study. The following narrowly limited definition of principles of learning was accepted:

> . . . generalizations, based on research findings, and generally accepted by learning theorists, which state positive relationships between certain environmental conditions which can be manipulated by the teacher, and the acquisition, retention and/or transfer, by learners in school situations, of facts, concepts, or generalizations.

The primary purpose of the study was investigation of the following hypothesis:

> If a student teacher is guided in analyzing his verbal teaching behavior by means of a list of selected learning principles, to the end that he will make commitments to implement principles of learning, then the verbal teaching behavior of the student teacher will increasingly indicate the implementation of these same learning principles.

Source and Operational Definitions
of Principles of Learning

Many generalizations about learning meeting the terms of the definition above were found. In the interests of practicality, a selection had to be made. Criteria for selection were devised and accepted. The following criteria were employed in selecting the particular generalizations used in the study:

1. The statements must express relationships upon which learning theorists are in agreement.

2. Particular attention was to be given to the ideas of motivation, retention, and transfer.

3. The number of principles was to be sufficiently limited to be remembered easily, but no large portion of a lesson should be neglected.

4. There must be likelihood that the principles selected could be implemented by student teachers in elementary school classrooms, within the organizational pattern established by the cooperating teacher.

5. Principles selected should contribute to increasing understanding by student teachers of individual differences among learners.

Several statements of agreement among learning theorists were studied. Use of the criteria for selection resulted in identification of seven major ideas, which became the principles used in the study.

The final step was restatement of these agreements in a form developed for the study. In order to make the generalizations identified into "power principles"[1] it was necessary to establish two key terms in each statement, and indicate the relationship between them.

While in each statement one term might have been _learning_, caution suggested use of the phrase, _chances of learning_. The other key term was the condition known to be favorable to learning, so described as to supply a clue or suggest an implication concerning teacher behavior, since teacher behavior was perceived as one cause for existence of the favorable condition. Finally, the descriptive relationship between the learner's

---

[1]Finley Carpenter and Eugene E. Haddan, _Systematic Application of Psychology to Education_ (New York: The MacMillan Company, 1964), pp. 34-37.

chances of learning and the teacher's behavior in creating a condition favorable for learning was stated positively, but in terms of probability rather than certainty.

Out of this process there evolved the following list of seven statements:

1. Learning is facilitated when the learner responds actively in the learning situation.

2. A learner's chances of learning are increased when his purposes and those of the teacher are sufficiently similar for him to perceive the relationship.

3. A learner's chances of learning are increased when the material to be learned is meaningful to him.

4. A learner's chances of learning are increased when he can see some possibility of succeeding in the learning task he is attempting.

5. A learner's chances of learning are increased each time he experiences success in a learning task.

6. A learner's chances of learning are increased when he has opportunities for and assistance in the discovery of facts, relationships, and generalizations.

7. Possibility of the retention of learned material is increased when the learner practices his learning immediately, frequently, and in varied situations.

During the orientation sessions that preceded data collection, the student teachers reviewed their knowledge and their ideas about the conditions of learning. They examined these principles, with some of their implications for teacher behavior, and they developed tag names or abbreviations by which the statements would later be identified. Deeper understanding of the principles and further applications would develop through conferences.

Content and Procedures of Conferences as
the Setting for Teaching by Supervisors

Each supervisory conference was preceded by individual analysis of
the typescript of the previously recorded teaching session. While the
process of analysis required thoughtful consideration both of the record
and of the significance of the ideas of the system of analysis, the process
of recording the analysis was a simple one.

Analysis of typescripts. The procedure employed was the following:

1. Read the entire typescript.

2. Reread the first page.

3. Try to identify on the first page the use of a principle,
    or failure to use a principle when it would have been
    appropriate.

4. Circle the identified segment of the page. In the margin,
    write the name or number of the principle identified, with
    the value symbol.

5. Continue this process throughout the typescript.

6. In situations in which more than one principle seem
    operative, try to decide upon the one most clearly
    visible. If the decision seems very difficult,
    record both.

The value symbol referred to above was use of the plus (+) sign
to indicate effective use of the principle indicated by name or number,
and the name or number with a minus (-) sign to indicate failure to use
or violation of a principle.

With the first conferences, one of the most conspicuous features
of the completed study began to be evident, as differences among the
supervisors became visible.

Differences among supervisors. While common guidelines for
conferences had been accepted, the investigators had believed that

conference style was and should be characteristic of the individual supervisor. Differences in style immediately became evident. These differences were so wide and so consistent as to defy easy description; they suggest a focus for later study.

Consistent differences emerged in the form of commitments stated by student teachers in different supervisory groups, the time of their statement, the number stated by the student teacher as contrasted with the number suggested by the supervisor, the principles given most attention in each supervisory group, the frequency of statement and restatement of commitments, and the principles of learning concerning which commitment were stated. While all these differences might have been expected among the nine student teachers, the patterns of difference that were evident suggested differences among the supervisors as the principal cause.

A third aspect of difference among the supervisors was noticeable in their varying perceptions of the meaning, the applicability, the flexibility of and interrelationships among the selected learning principles. This difference, like that of individual style, was probably inescapable.

Among differences that appeared, one remarkable likeness became visible.

Common emphasis on student teachers' concerns. The supervisors shared concern lest the value of the student teachers' total experience be in any way lessened through their involvement in the research. One of the accepted guidelines stressed the importance of listening to and showing respect for the student teacher. Analysis of typescripts revealed many topics which might well have been discussed in conferences, which time would not permit. Out of all these conditions, topics selected for discussion in conferences were, almost without exception, those about which concern was shown or questions raised by the student teachers. While the supervisors' concerns were not disregarded, it was found that they very frequently paralleled or were included in topics suggested by the student teachers.

The spontaneous development of this pattern by all the supervisors, and the difference from the more usual supervisor-centered procedure of analysis, evaluation, and advice became a notable feature of the study.

Discussions in conferences ranged widely. It would be difficult to describe a typical conference discussion based on principles.

Discussion based on principles. Most of the student teachers had little previous study of educational psychology, and their exposure to the selected principles during their orientation period was brief indeed. The intention of the supervisors was "to help them clarify principles . . . to extend and deepen their understanding of what principles mean when applied to the guidance of learning."[1]

Individual differences, both of supervisors and of student teachers, were clearly evident in the ways they approached this task. Some part of every conference, however, dealt with principles of learning, their use or possible use by the student teacher, or their meaning in a particular situation.

Differences were apparent in the ways discussions were carried on,

---

[1]Florence Stratemeyer and Margaret Lindsey, Working with Student Teachers (New York: Bureau of Publications, Teachers College, Columbia University, 1958), p. 259.

in the specific principles considered, and in the applications that were identified. Some conferences included the topic of use of principles of learning as one of many topics considered. Others focused on the use of principles of learning as a means of solving specific teaching problems of student teachers. Some considerations of the topic were brief and rather casual, others were concentrated and in depth.

Special interests of individual supervisors were reflected in the number of principles discussed and the emphasis given each. Two supervisors appeared to give nearly equal attention to each of the seven principles. The third seemed to give special attention to the ideas of purpose, meaning, and discovery.

Behavior identified as use of a principle varied also, among the student teachers and among the supervisors. The kinds of behavior considered changed in each case during the period of the study.

While the only statement that can truly be made concerning all the discussions based on principles is that such discussions did occur, it can be said that all conference participants found it possible to analyze teaching by means of this procedure, and for the student teachers to make commitments to change their behavior based on this system of analysis.

Commitments based on principles. While different emphases were evident in supervisory groups, in every case commitments for changed behavior emerged from conference discussion. Commitments made were both within and out of the system of analysis, but those within the system predominated.

In one group, commitments were made and recorded throughout discussions. Many of these were suggested by the supervisor. In another group, every commitment was stated by the student teachers, every one at the end of a conference. In the third group both procedures were used.

All selected principles were discussed at some time during the study and at least three statements of commitment made concerning each. The ideas of meaning and discovery were each the subject of eight commitments, probably because of emphasis placed on these principles by one supervisor. Restatements of commitment were distributed as widely and with the same emphases.

Two kinds of statements within the system were evident. Some commitments were to the use of described behavior, identified as being use of one of the principles. Other commitments were to use of one of the principles, with alternative kinds of behavior described. These differences were consistent within supervisory groups.

In most cases student teachers made commitments willingly. In one case, in which the student teacher apparently saw little possibility of doing differently, commitments were made reluctantly. There appeared to be a relationship between a student teacher's perception of his teaching situation and his willingness to make commitments to changed behavior.

Differences among supervisors, evidenced by student teachers' commitments as by other aspects of the study, were a conspicuous and unsolicited finding of the study.

Findings of the Study

The first condition of the hypothesis of the study was fulfilled:

If a student teacher is guided in analyzing his verbal teaching behavior by means of a list of selected learning principles to the end that he will make commitments to implement principles of learning. . . .

The nine student teachers made forty-two initial statements of commitment, of which thirty-eight were within the system of analysis. They made twenty-five restatements, of which twenty-four were within the system. Of sixty-two statements and restatements within the system of analysis, fifty-nine were related to specific principles on the selected list.

Student teachers could be guided in analyzing their verbal teaching behavior by means of a list of selected principles of learning. They could make commitments to implement these learning principles.

Findings concerning the second condition were less clear:

. . . the verbal teaching behavior of the student teacher will increasingly indicate the implementation of these same learning principles.

In order to discover whether there was increasing implementation of principles, it was necessary to assume that implementation of commitments concerning principles was equivalent to implementation of principles. Thus, evidence of implementation of commitments related to specific principles was sought in each teaching session following statement of the commitment.

Of initial statements of commitment related to specific principles, 74 percent were implemented in the teaching session immediately following their statement.

Of statements and restatements of commitment related to specific principles 83.1 percent were implemented in the teaching session immediately following the statement or restatement.

As the total number of statements and restatements increased throughout the study, the total number of instances of implementation also increased, but at a slower rate. Therefore, the percent of implementation decreased irregularly from cycle to cycle.

If evidence of increasing implementation of principles of learning is defined in terms of percent of implementation found in each cycle, the hypothesis of the study is not supported by the data. If the overall increase from cycle to cycle in number of teaching sessions in which implementation was found is accepted as satisfying the meaning of "increasingly implement," the hypothesis is supported.

Other findings were identified. There was little difference in implementation of commitments suggested by the supervisor and those initiated by the student teacher, and the very small difference favored those suggested by the supervisor. The greatest percent of implementation was of commitments concerning the ideas of experience of success and of repetition. The smallest percent of implementation was of commitments concerning the possibility of success.

Data of the study, when analyzed in terms of commitments made and their implementation, do not fully support the hypothesis. There was evidence that student teachers were able (1) to analyze and discuss their teaching behavior in terms of the selected principles; (2) to make commitments to implement these principles; and (3) to implement many of these commitments in subsequent teaching sessions.

Other significant ideas emerged from the study. The value of planned conferences, beginning with a real concern, using an agreed upon system of analysis, and closing with plans for future action has been demonstrated. Collaborative research has been proved possible. Research within on-going programs of teacher preparation has been found to be feasible. The particular system of analysis proved itself flexible, adaptable to different situations and problems, and usable by college supervisors and student teachers with different perceptions and different problems.

The most significant result of the study was in the number and kind of questions that it raised, which formed the basis of later, more sophisticated studies.

Verbal Behavior as the Basis for Analysis of
Teaching[1] in Supervisory Conferences

The importance of language in teaching and learning is readily recognized. Along with the pervasive quality of verbal behavior in teaching is the teacher's ability to control and change that behavior. Attention to verbal behavior, the researchers reasoned, would be an important way to help the student teacher improve his teaching. The supervisory conference is a central factor in tutoring the student teacher.

The investigators hypothesized that student teachers who examined their teaching in terms of a specified system would plan and implement changes in subsequent teaching encounters. Recorded typescripts of five teaching and five conference sessions provided data on each of nine student teachers who were the subjects of this study.

---

[1]Anna Beth Brown, Margaret Cobban, and Floyd Waterman, "An Analysis of Verbal Teaching Behavior: An Approach to Supervisory Conferences with Student Teachers" (unpublished Ed.D. Project Report, Teachers College, Columbia University, New York, 1965).

The System for Analysis

Several of the available systems for analyzing verbal interaction were considered, but the investigators wanted one that would be applicable for student use. They decided, therefore, to modify and adapt the system of Bellack and associates.[1]

Pedagogical moves. The game aspects of teaching stimulated Bellack and associates to develop a description of classroom interaction with a focus upon the way teachers and pupils play the language game. Teachers hold the authority in the classroom and usually make the first "move" by setting the pace for the lesson. Once he has set the stage for learning activities, the teacher asks a question and pupils begin to respond; so begins the ping-pong character of classroom discourse.

Bellack described the pedagogical moves as either initiatory or reflexive. The former are structuring and soliciting. Definitions of the pedagogical moves follow:

> Structuring. Structuring moves serve the pedagogical functions of focusing attention on subject matter or classroom procedures and launching interaction between students and teachers. They set the context for subsequent behavior or performance. For example, teachers frequently begin a class period with a structuring move in which they focus attention on the topic or problem to be discussed during the session.

> Soliciting. Moves in this category are designed to elicit a verbal response, encourage persons addressed to attend to something, or elicit a physical response. All genuine questions are solicitations, as are commands, imperatives, and requests.

---

[1]Arno A. Bellack, Joel R. Davitz et al., The Language of the Classroom, U.S. Office of Education Cooperative Research Project No. 1497 (New York: Institute of Psychological Research, Teachers College, Columbia University, 1963).

Responding. These moves bear a reciprocal relationship to soliciting moves and occur only in relation to them. Their pedagogical function is to fulfill the expectation of soliciting moves. Thus, students' answers to teachers' questions are classified as responding moves.

Reacting. These moves are occasioned by a structuring, soliciting, responding, or another reacting move, but are not directly elicited by them. Pedagogically, these moves serve to shape or mold classroom discourse by accepting, rejecting, modifying or expanding what has been said previously. Reacting moves differ from responding moves, in that while a responding move is always directly elicited by a solicitation, preceding moves serve only as the occasion for reactions. Evaluation by a teacher of a student's response, for example, is designated a reacting move.[1]

Student teachers, the investigators felt, could examine classroom interaction by use of Bellack's pedagogical moves and become more aware of their language and its role in setting the stage for interaction. This much of the Bellack system could be adopted and used by student teachers within a very short training period. The pedagogical moves pointed quickly to the functions of the verbal behavior but the analysis was yet incomplete.

Cognitive processes of pupils. The researchers wanted to focus upon the cognitive as Baldwin stressed the need in her report:

Measures of the behaviors presently used in observational studies on both teachers and children have been restricted primarily to social-emotional and motivational factors. There are almost no studies of the subject matter content of teacher-child interactions or the way teachers actually present new information, answer questions, or encourage a search for underlying principles. These behaviors should relate to pupils' cognitive development. . . .[2]

---

[1]Ibid., pp. 6-7.

[2]Clara P. Baldwin, "Naturalistic Studies of Classroom Learning," Review of Educational Research, 35:111-112, April, 1965.

70

The pedagogical moves, the researchers felt, met the need for a study of the "way teachers actually present new information and answer questions," but the encouragement of pupils "to search for underlying principles" seemed uncovered by the moves. Both Taba[1] and Miller[2] had developed some schemes for charting pupil thinking, but they seemed too complicated for use with students. Therefore, the researchers decided to develop a crude set of cognitive categories to add to the pedagogical moves as a basis for analysis of classroom teaching.

In constructing the cognitive categories, thought processes of a similar order were grouped together into a single cluster. The cognitive processes developed are as follows:

1. Perceiving, recalling, recognizing. The speaker selects certain stimuli from his environment through the use of his senses and brings them to the conscious level by verbal description. He calls back to memory by recollecting observations from previous experience. He is aware that the conditions observed are the same as those previously known.

2. Discriminating, comparing, defining. The speaker selects distinguishing features from the more general features of ideas or phenomena; he examines for similarities; he names, describes, or states his perception of the general and specific features of ideas or phenomena.

3. Classifying, relating, generalizing. The speaker puts together groups of ideas, events, and situations that have characteristics in common. He shows the connection between one situation and another and views the situation

---

[1]Hilda Taba, Samuel Leving, and Freeman F. Elzey, Thinking in Elementary School Children, U.S. Office of Education Cooperative Research Project No. 1574 (San Francisco: San Francisco State College, 1964), p. iv.

[2]George L. Miller, Assessing Pupil Mental Activity in Classroom Discussion: A Manual for Coding Pupil Comments (Salt Lake City: William M. Stewart School, University of Utah, 1964), p. 3.

as a whole by combining ideas, events, and elements into a unified statement.

4. <u>Opining, judging, evaluating</u>. The speaker holds a conclusion with confidence but it is not always based upon extensive evidence. He deliberates and asserts his decision on the basis of some criteria; he appraises carefully and makes quantitative decisions using criteria.

5. <u>Inferring, interpreting, applying</u>. The speaker surmises probable consequences through reasoning. He translates previous experience or ideas into new forms, and he employs for a particular purpose a previous idea, or he makes a connection by bringing to bear previous experience.

Two other categories proved to be necessary to code all of the classroom discourse appropriately. Some statements were designed merely to facilitate interaction. They included the pupil talk that is repeated by the teacher when she feels that the child has not been heard. These statements and most of the management talk, such as "Please close the door," were grouped into a category identified as <u>facilitating talk</u>.

There were times when the tape recorder was not able to pick up some of the interaction. This was caused by extraneous sounds that interfered with the taping, or by several children speaking together which resulted in a garbled sound, or by a child's voice being so soft that it could not be recorded. Thus the need for the category <u>non-codable</u>.

The two non-cognitive categories are described as follows:

6. <u>Facilitating talk</u>. This category and the next category are clearly not part of the cognitive processes. This category is used to classify talk which is intended to facilitate interaction in the classroom. It includes mere repetition which is given so others may hear. It also includes the simple supportive statement ("Umm," "O.K.," "Yes," "Fine," or "Good") when it is clear that no judgment is being made. Most of the routines or management talk such as "Please close the door" fall under this category.

7. <u>Non-codable</u>. This category is necessitated by
inaudible statements or comments which are incomplete
or so garbled that their meaning cannot be inferred.

Equipped with the moves to identify the pedagogical intent of the
verbal behavior and the categories to indicate the inferred cognitive
processes of children, the college supervisors trained student teachers
to analyze their verbal teaching behavior and to plan, during supervisory
conferences, for improved behavior in subsequent teaching sessions.

Analysis as the Basis for
Conferring with Student Teachers

Employment of the pedagogical moves and cognitive categories as
bases for discourse introduced certain unique features in the conferences.
The investigators also used supervisory practices applicable to any conference. The supervisory conference is a teaching-learning situation.
As was true in the study reported just previously, style differences
among college supervisors were assumed and use of the system of analysis
was not intended as a limitation upon style. Basic recognition of communication and human relation skills was an underlying assumption of all
supervisors. The conference guidelines detailed on page 56 were accepted
by the researchers.

Use of the pedagogical moves and the cognitive categories necessitated training in the system of analysis. For the college supervisors
training in coding according to pedagogical moves and cognitive categories
began during the pilot study.[1] Experience in coding typescripts continued

_____

[1]Anna Rockhill, "An Exploratory Study: Two Types of Student Teacher-
Supervisor Conferences Based Upon Verbal Teaching Behavior" (unpublished
Ed.D. project report, Teachers College, Columbia University, New York,
1965).

as materials were prepared for eventual use in orientation meetings with student teachers.

When the student teacher-subjects were selected, a three-day session was conducted to train student teachers in use of the system of analysis. The student teacher's task was defined as (1) planning his teaching; (2) teaching; (3) conferring with the college supervisor; (4) using new insights in planning for the next teaching session; and (5) teaching again. These tasks formed a cycle that would be repeated four times during the course of the study. The purpose of the conference, the student-teacher subjects were told, was to help them decide how to change and improve their teaching behavior in sessions subsequent to the conferences.

Both college supervisors and student teachers were required to prepare for the supervisory conference by coding the typescript. To assure a degree of skill in coding, before embarking upon analysis of their own teaching, student teachers identified moves and cognitive categories in several typescripts. College supervisors helped the student teachers with practice in coding.

The coding scheme was a series of abbreviations representing (a) the identification of the speaker; (b) the pedagogical move performed by the teacher (student teacher); (c) the cognitive processes elicited from pupils; and (d) the number of lines of talk within a pedagogical move. Thus margins of typescripts were independently coded by both supervisors and student teachers. For example, a passage coded, T.SOL/2/3, would be interpreted as follows: T indicates the student teacher was speaking; the student teacher was performing the <u>soliciting</u> move (SOL);

his solicitation seemed to be eliciting a cognitive process within Category Two--discriminating, comparing, defining (2); and the move consisted of three lines of teacher talk (3).

By the end of the three days, student teachers and college supervisors were able to achieve substantial agreement on the coding process. Student teachers were placed in schools and began working with typescripts of their own teaching sessions. As illustrated in the excerpts which follow, however, training continued throughout the entire study.

CS:[1]   Look at line four. You say, "Why can the candle burn longer in the jack-o-lantern?" You are asking for a generalization there, aren't you? The pupils came back with partial answers. One child said, "Because it has holes in it." But in place of correcting him, you said, "They let the air in." And you summarized, "It lets in the air so the candle, which needs air to burn, can burn longer." So what you have actually done is to get them to do some of the generalizing through the questions you asked.

ST:[2]   I always think it is better when they say something. To take that and tie it on to something else; tie it together rather than completely disregard it, because it does mean something to them. When he said that it has holes in it, he was saying something. They don't quite explain the whole thing--what holes have to do with the candle.

CS: That is because he is still trying to verbalize these understandings. Because you sensed that he understood, you kept your question going in the right direction to ask for more of the generalization. So you see, you have a lot of control over the soliciting that you use.

In a more carefully controlled study continuance of training might be considered a flaw in the research design. This study, however, was

---

[1]Letters CS indicate college supervisor speaking.

[2]Letters ST indicate student teacher speaking.

largely exploratory in nature; neither the coding nor the training processes were ends in themselves. The coded typescripts were the vehicles for analysis of the teaching. The intent of the analysis was that of understanding and controlling verbal teaching behavior. Supervisory conferences were to result in plans or "next steps" in future teaching. Although student teachers were never told this, the college supervisors sought to elicit commitments for definite action in subsequent teaching sessions.

The researchers defined a commitment as a statement of intent to act in future teaching. It was agreed that a commitment could be stated by the student teacher or by the college supervisor. If commitments were stated by college supervisors, they sought ways of insuring that it had been actively accepted by the student teacher.[1]

It was only natural that the language of the system of analysis appear (either explicitly or implicitly) in the statement of commitments. The conference excerpt which follows is an example of a commitment which resulted when the college supervisor complimented the student teacher on the type of soliciting used in a previous lesson. Category Four--opining, judging, evaluating--is implied in the discussion.

CS: You asked a lot of very good questions in this lesson
. . . wherein you sought opinions. I mentioned the one
that you cut off with a second question. . . . Do you
see opportunities for doing more of this kind of thing
in the future lessons?

ST: Of cutting it off?

CS: No, no [laughed]. We find those opportunities

---

[1]See page 54.

automatically. We don't have to look for them. I
meant more opportunities to avoid it--providing more
opportunities for children to give opinions and
reactions.

ST: Oh, I think I'll be more conscious of it.

CS: This would be one of the things you want to be more
conscious of?

ST: Yes.

Still another excerpt from a supervisory conference not only

illustrates the use of the language of analysis but also shows how a

college supervisor used the coded typescript to help a student teacher

analyze his teaching sessions:

CS: Did you expect more in the way of generalizing than
you got?

ST: I realized after reading the typescript that this was
all they could do. I think a few were able to say that
no matter where the items were put, they all added up
to five. But the other children couldn't do this.

CS: Do you think that some of the other children had the
same understanding?

ST: I don't think they did.

CS: Let me put it another way. Do you think they had an
understanding that no matter where they placed the
object--

ST: Yes, yes, I do think they understand that, because
of their responses. But I don't think that most
were ready to try to draw a generalization.

Some of the commitments emerged from direct questions of college

supervisors. In one conference, for example, the supervisor asked, "Are

you going to try to have the children infer, or interpret, or make

application [Cognitive Category Five]?" "Yes," replied the student

teacher. "I always try to do that but I need to make a more deliberate effort to do it." By itself, such a statement could not be considered a commitment. However, other supporting statements throughout the conference substantiated the student teacher's acceptance of the commitment as his own. Commitments such as "helping pupils do their own generalizing," "structuring a few concepts," "soliciting and structuring for a variety of cognitive processes," "involving more children," "structuring the beginning of the lesson," "avoid cutting off children's comments," and "help children to opine and to interpret," were typical of those which came out of the supervisory conferences.

Findings of the Study

Data from the nine student teachers' teaching and conferring sessions relate to two dimensions of teaching: the type and amount of interaction in the classrooms and the statement and implementation of commitments. The findings reflect the influence of the system of analysis upon the verbal teaching behavior of student teachers.

The dual classification of language made it possible to talk with student teachers about their verbal behavior and the type of thinking they seemed to elicit from children. Analysis of the pedagogical moves showed that student teachers, like their elders in the profession, did most of the talking in the classroom. Moreover, 60.3 percent of the moves by student teachers were solicitations and only 3.5 percent were classified as reacting moves. Pupil talk, on the other hand was almost entirely, 74.3 percent, responding.

Classification of the inferred cognitive processes of pupils also provided an interesting picture. Category One—perceiving, recalling, recognizing--accounted for 37.1 percent of the pupil moves and Category Two--discriminating, comparing, defining--for 15.6 percent. Together, these categories accounted for 52.7 percent of the pupil moves in the classroom. Predominance of pupil moves in these categories suggests teaching centered upon recall and definition of facts. Only 5.7 percent of the pupil moves in this study fell into Category Five--inferring, interpreting, applying.

The other findings were related to the number and type of commitments and their implementation in subsequent teaching sessions. Among the nine student teachers, fifty-five separate commitments were developed in the supervisory conferences. Twenty-two, or 40 percent, were stated in the first conferences and an additional thirteen, or 23.6 percent, were stated in the second conference. In addition, every student teacher restated at least one of his commitments. In all, twenty-one, or 38.1 percent, of the total commitments were restated one or more times. Most of the commitments (65.4 percent) were stated by the student teachers; the balance were suggested by college supervisors.

Implementation of commitments in subsequent teaching sessions was determined on a simple "Yes" or "No" basis. The presence of teaching behavior in the lesson which seemed to implement the commitment, was the criterion for the "Yes" evaluation. College supervisors exchanged typescripts to seek evidence of implementation and as a check against their own analyses. On the whole, student teachers tended to implement a high percentage of their commitments but the five teaching sessions (from which data were gathered) may be a restricting factor which could, in part, negate the high record of implementation (85.4 percent).

The findings sustain the hypothesis that student teachers who examine their teaching in terms of pedagogical moves and cognitive categories would plan and implement changes in subsequent teaching sessions. The investigators conceived this as an exploratory study from which findings might generate new questions and unsolved problems.

Implications for Study of Supervision as Teaching

In the two preceding sections, related team efforts have been described. One focused upon helping student teachers examine their teaching in terms of selected principles of learning. The other approach focused upon the teaching act by classifying verbal behavior in terms of pedagogical moves and the cognitive processes they seem to elicit from pupils. While both approaches make implicit reference to the affective aspects of classroom interaction, their major stress is upon the verbal behavior of the teacher.

The most potent implication of these studies is that student teachers respond favorably to systematic analysis of their teaching. Additionally, they viewed the application of specific systems of analysis as an effective learning procedure.

Researchers using principles of learning as bases for analysis believed that student teachers should have been involved in selecting appropriate principles and that once they had been exposed to extensive study of the psychology of learning, students could select and state their own set of principles. Cognitive categories selected by the researchers for the other study were not ordered into an hierarchy. Yet student teachers consistently viewed them in this manner. An implication here is that students should be more involved in developing, utilizing, and modifying systems of analysis.

It is conceivable that no one system should be used in a "pure form" but rather a synthesis developed by all parties in the supervisory process--the student teacher, the college supervisor, and the cooperating teacher. Certainly Heidelbach's[1] comments, about the limitations of existing approaches to the study of teaching, should be taken into account as one plans a program. Perhaps the greatest value of a system of analysis rests not in specifics of the system, but in the sense of awareness it provides the student.

Supervisory approaches and research thereon which do not take into account the regular classroom teacher as well as the college supervisor and student teacher are inadequate for the task. College supervisors need to work with cooperating school personnel to help them understand the specialized instructional process in the supervisory conference. Of course, college supervisors must critically examine their own conferring procedures and styles. The dynamics of the supervisory system is appropriate material for research and exploration.

These two studies serve to emphasize the value of objective records as the bases for conferences. Increased use of audio and video tape recorders should be explored, but written notes or participation grids and/or interaction charts should not be overlooked. Inquiry should be made into the influences of college supervisor's style. A related question worthy of research would be that of tracing development of style

---

[1]Chapter II.

or changes in conferring procedures employed by either a college supervisor or a cooperating teacher.

A new dimension in the education of teachers is direct experience
components which are conducted in non-school agencies. Community agencies
(both private and governmental) are often providing different services
which are educative and from which students would profit. Perhaps an
early involvement in research efforts would be fruitful. Commercial
organizations associated with computer-assisted instruction and systems
analysis must be consulted and their support gained if all phases of the
supervisory process are to be studied. Simulated experiences are becoming
common for student teachers and research should be designed while they are
in the developmental stages.

Staff arrangements for student teaching need serious overhauling
in most teacher education institutions. One of the implications of the
two-phase study reported here is the need for colleges to look at the
number of student teachers assigned to a supervisor. College supervisors
cannot work adequately with cooperating teachers and student teachers if
they are overloaded.

A related matter is time reserved for conference preparation.
Systems approaches to conferences require more time and while most
universities recognize this for regular lecture sessions, they have yet
to provide adequate time allotments for conference preparation. Certainly
there are budget considerations in all of these matters, but the matter
becomes all the more crucial when one looks at the off-campus centers for
student teaching which are developing around the country. Exporting
college supervisors and/or clinical professors to off-center centers in no

way reduces the need for careful planning and adequate provisions for staff with the time and facilities to function in a broader role of supervision.

Increased utilization of audio and video recordings suggests the need for both space and personnel for the operation, maintenance, and storage of such equipment. Special viewing areas and adequate office space should be planned at the time that decisions for utilization are made. Overcrowded office conditions will greatly detract from effective conferences.

Finally, administrators must recognize the need to provide staff, budget, and facilities to conduct research and evaluation of the supervisory conferring process. The study of the process is appropriate content for research by teacher educators and is of interest to all students of teaching.

Chapter IV

A PROMISSORY MODEL FOR ANALYZING AND DESCRIBING VERBAL
INTERACTION BETWEEN COLLEGE SUPERVISORS AND STUDENT
TEACHERS DURING SUPERVISORY CONFERENCES[1]

Richard Verne Brown and Miriam Schaad Hoffman

Individualized conferences between student teachers and college
supervisors represent a significant part of the supervision of student
teachers. The purpose of individualized conferences is to provide
guidance for teachers by assisting them in analyzing and diagnosing their
teaching behavior as a means of modifying that behavior in light of new
knowledge.

Key persons in individualized conferences are college supervisors.
To a great extent the effectiveness of conferences depends upon their
teaching behavior. If the teaching behavior of college supervisors is
crucial in the guidance of student teachers, then it is important for
supervisors to analyze and diagnose their teaching behavior in order to
achieve insights into their teaching processes as a means of planning

---

[1]Richard Verne Brown and Miriam Schaad Hoffman, "A Promissory Model
for Analyzing and Describing Verbal Interaction Between College Supervisors
and Student Teachers During Supervisory Conferences" (unpublished Ed.D.
report, Teachers College, Columbia University, 1967).

modifications in their own behavior. An analytic tool which would enable supervisors to examine their teaching behavior in conferences should be worthwhile.

Typescripts can provide supervisors with detailed records of their behavior in individualized conferences. Unfortunately, these typescripts are meaningless unless supervisors have conceptual tools which will help them analyze and interpret their behavior as revealed in the typescripts. Various schemes for analyzing classroom behavior have been proposed by Aschner,[1] Bellack et al.,[2] Amidon and Flanders,[3] Smith and Meux,[4] and others. The relevancy of these conceptual tools for analyzing and describing the teaching behavior of college supervisors in individualized conferences is unknown.

The purpose of this study was to develop a conceptual tool, i.e., promissory model, for analyzing and describing the verbal interaction between college supervisors and student teachers during supervisory conferences. Such a tool can assist college supervisors by providing

[1]Mary Jane Aschner, "The Analysis of Verbal Interaction in the Classroom," Theory and Research in Teaching, Arno Bellack, editor (New York: Bureau of Publications, Teachers College, Columbia University, 1963), pp. 53-78.

[2]Arno A. Bellack et al., The Language of the Classroom, U.S. Office of Education Cooperative Research Project, No. 1497 (New York: Institute of Psychological Research, Teachers College, Columbia University, 1963).

[3]Edmund J. Amidon and Ned A. Flanders, The Role of the Teacher in the Classroom (Minneapolis, Minnesota: Paul S. Amidon and Associates, 1963).

[4]B. Othanel Smith and Milton O. Meux, A Study of the Logic of Teaching (Urbana, Illinois: Bureau of Educational Research, College of Education, University of Illinois, 1963).

them with a scientific base for examining their teaching behavior in order
to improve their guidance of student teachers.

Research Procedures

The research procedures employed in developing the promissory
model for analyzing and describing the verbal teaching behavior of college
supervisors in their individualized conferences with student teachers was
based upon the analytic activity described by McClellan and Komisar as
"rational reconstruction."

> . . . Rational reconstruction has three phases: the first
> is to abstract essential elements from some specific intel-
> lectual activity; the second is to establish certain formal
> categories or relations among these abstract elements with,
> perhaps, explicit rules for moves in the schema; the third
> is to apply the resulting scheme or model reflexively as a
> basis for guiding or criticizing the conduct of the original
> activity from which the abstraction began.[1]

The overall design resembled the first two phases of rational
reconstruction and consisted of: (1) identifying and abstracting from
the literature on counseling and general school supervision the dimensions
of performance[2] of counselors and supervisors in their conferring
function; (2) analyzing and classifying the identified dimensions of
performance into categories; (3) arranging the categories in order to
form a category system; (4) defining and testing the categories within the

---

[1]James E. McClellan and B. Paul Komisar, "Preface to the American
Edition," Truth and Fallacy in Educational Theory, Charles D. Hardie,
author (New York: Bureau of Publications, Teachers College, Columbia
University, 1962), p. vi.

[2]Dimensions of performance are activities or characteristics of
activities which are utilized by counselors and supervisors in their
conferring function.

category system; and (5) postulating the category system as the promissory model and describing the interrelationships among the categories within the model.

Analysis of Literature on
General Supervision and Counseling

In selecting literature for analysis, it was assumed that, although the primary focus of the individualized conference is on instructional problems, the college supervisor needs to provide an optimum emotional climate. Therefore, it seemed apropos to analyze literature in the areas of general school supervision and counseling which pertained to the dyadic situation in order to identify and abstract the dimensions of performance of counselors and supervisors in their conferring functions. The literature selected contained dimensions of performance which were related to both the improvement of instruction and the development of a satisfactory emotional climate.

The major category for the analysis of the literature was the dimensions of performance in the conferring function. After deductively analyzing the literature, 194 cases of dimensions of performance were identified.

Analysis and Synthesis of Dimensions of
Performance into a Promissory Model

In order to analyze and synthesize the 194 dimensions of performance identified through analysis of the literature on counseling and general school supervision, it was necessary to implement the second phase of rational reconstruction, i.e., the establishment of formal categories which subsumed the dimensions of performance.

Identification of discrete cases. Initial examination of the 194 dimensions of performance revealed repetitious and inappropriate cases. Therefore, prior to classifying the cases into categories through inductive processes, it was necessary to examine the dimensions of performance, identify those cases deemed discrete and appropriate for purpose of this study, and omit repetitious and inappropriate cases. Two criteria were developed to facilitate this task: (1) cases retained were required to be unique from all other cases and (2) cases retained were required to be capable of being identified through inference on typescripts.

After typing the 194 cases of dimensions of performance on three-by-five cards the first criterion was applied to the cases by (1) placing those cases whose syntactical structure and content were identical or nearly identical on the same stack; (2) identifying and retaining a single representative case; and (3) omitting duplications of the criterion case. The second criterion was applied by omitting cases which were not capable of being identified on conference typescripts. One hundred twenty-three dimensions of performance remained as appropriate cases to be utilized in hypothesizing categories.

Classification of cases into categories. The next phase in the development of the promissory model was inductive synthesis of appropriate and discrete cases into category procedures. Cases which formed a category procedure were required to contain (1) common themes and (2) common operations. Common themes refer to the foci of cases whereas common operations refer to particular acts employed in carrying out procedures dealing with a specific theme. Category procedures are derived from cases

<u>of dimensions of performance which contain common themes and common</u>

<u>operations</u>. The 123 cases of dimensions of performance were first sorted into stacks containing common themes and then the cases within each stack were classified on the basis of common operations dealing with the same theme. The following eleven category procedures were identified.

Administrative procedures

Catharsis procedures

Controlling procedures

Defining procedures

Hypothesizing procedures

Identifying procedures

Interpreting-evaluating procedures

Leading procedures

Rapport building procedures

Social amenities procedures

Summary procedures

<u>Organization of categories into a category system</u>. As a means of identifying and describing the relationship among the eleven category procedures as well as organizing them into a system, category procedures were synthesized by an inductive process into classes and the classes were ordered. The following criterion was used to synthesize category procedures into category processes: category procedures which were to form a category process were required to contain common themes and inter-dependent operations. Common themes refer to mutual foci of category procedures whereas interdependent operations refer to reciprocal sets of

acts utilized in carrying out a category process. <u>Category processes are</u>
<u>derived from category procedures containing common themes and inter-</u>
<u>dependent operations</u>.

After implementing the criterion to synthesize category procedures
into category processes by identifying common themes and interdependent
operations, the following process conceptualizations evolved. Administrative and summary procedures were synthesized into routine processes;
controlling and leading procedures were synthesized into directing processes; identifying and defining procedures were synthesized into comprehending processes; interpreting-evaluation procedures and hypothesizing
procedures were synthesized into analyzing processes. Interdependent
operations for rapport building, catharsis, and social amenities procedures
were not identified. At this point the evolving category system appeared
as follows:

Routine processes

      Administrative procedures
      Summary procedures

Directing processes

      Leading procedures
      Controlling procedures

Comprehending processes

      Identifying procedures
      Defining procedures

Analyzing processes

      Interpreting-evaluating procedures
      Hypothesizing procedures

      Rapport building procedures
      Catharsis procedures
      Social amenities procedures

In order to further refine the evolving category system, the following criterion was developed to synthesize category processes and/or procedures into category domains: category processes and/or procedures which were to form a category domain were required to contain a common theme. In this instance a common theme refers to the major foci of the category processes and/or procedures. Category domains are derived from sets of category processes and/or procedures containing common themes.

Implementing the criterion to derive category domains resulted in the following conceptualizations. Comprehending and analyzing processes were synthesized into the problem solving domain; catharsis, rapport building, and social amenities procedures were synthesized into the affective domain; routine and directing processes were synthesized into the structuring domain. The following scheme represents these modifications:

Problem Solving Domain

Comprehending processes

> Identifying procedures
> Defining procedures

Analyzing processes

> Interpreting-evaluating procedures
> Hypothesizing procedures

Affective Domain

Catharsis procedures
Rapport building procedures
Social amenities procedures

Structuring Domain

Routine processes

    Administrative procedures
    Summary procedures

Directing processes

    Leading procedures
    Controlling procedures

<u>Definitions and behavioral illustrations of category system</u>. During
the next phase in the development of the promissory model the elements
within the category system were defined and tested. Category procedures
were defined by incorporating the defining terms representing the concepts
of the cases of dimensions of performance subsumed under the category
procedures. Definitions of the category processes were formulated by
incorporating the definitions of the category procedures subsumed under
them. Finally, category domains were defined by synthesizing the conceptualizations of the category processes or procedures subsumed under
them.

In addition to formulating definitions for each of the elements of
the category system, behavioral illustrations were provided for the procedural definitions. These illustrations depict the range of meaning
that can be ascribed to the definitions as well as provide a reality test
of the definitions of category procedures.

Problem Solving Domain

The problem solving domain includes comprehending and analyzing
processes. Included in this domain are those procedures which enable
conference participants to isolate and explicate the causal factors of

problems as well as those procedures which enable the participants to generalize solutions to problems by inferring relationships among the causal factors.

Comprehending Processes

Comprehending processes comprise identifying and defining procedures through which supervisors and/or teachers indicate an awareness of problems and move toward definition through translational procedures.

Identifying procedures. Identifying procedures involve methods whereby conference participants verbalize problems for discussion during conferences. Such statements or restatements merely indicate an awareness of existing difficulties.

Example

ST[1] One thing that was a problem was that each one had his magnet and that raised some conflicts; they didn't want to share them. They didn't want to share the object from the table; that was one problem.

Defining procedures. Defining procedures imply methods in which supervisors and/or teachers attempt to clarify problems through data-gathering techniques such as searching, investigating, questioning, advising, suggesting, and information giving. Supervisors and/or teachers attempt to obtain all necessary background information relevant to problems in order to identify pertinent causal factors. Defining procedures necessitate the translation of communications into concrete terms.

Example

ST   No, the sun doesn't turn but I tried to use the idea

_____

[1]In examples from typescripts, the initials "ST" refer to the student teacher and the initials "CS" refer to the college supervisor.

that you fix the light bulb so that they get the idea
that it was stable. When I showed the earth it was very
hard because the globe was not too big. I tried to show
the earth going and I moved it around but unfortunately
it was small; the children in back couldn't see it.

Analyzing Processes

Analyzing processes include those procedures through which conference participants attempt to gain insights into problems and to move
toward postulating solutions by determining major relationships among
identified causal factors and making predictions based upon these
relationships.

Interpreting-evaluating procedures. Interpreting-evaluating procedures involve attempts on the part of supervisors and/or teachers to
gain insight into problems by diagnosing and assessing performance in
terms of stated objectives. Included in these procedures are judgmental
statements and statements which propose that cause and effect relationships exist among various factors.

Example

CS I think this is certainly a valid comment in that
your own feelings of adequacy about a particular
subject will determine the extent to which you feel
free about letting children be comfortable, explore,
and make generalizations themselves. Maybe this
was a case of your making the generalizations for
them because you didn't want them to get further
than you felt comfortable.

Hypothesizing procedures. Hypothesizing procedures include
attempts of supervisors and/or teachers to postulate action hypotheses
based upon identified existing relationships among various factors. Such
procedures are concerned with putting plans and decisions into effect

94

and usually include statements related to lesson planning such as determining objectives, developing procedures, and programing.

<u>Example</u>

CS Do you see any way that you as a teacher could set the
    stage for these children to share? Let's pretend that
    you are using five magnets with these ten children and
    you want them to share. Do you think you could set the
    stage for that sharing?

ST Well, perhaps you could, as I said, give the magnets to
    five of the children if you only had five magnets and
    let them try one thing such as pick up one object. They
    can have their choice of anything, just one, and then
    give it to the next person to try. Have them on shifts.

Affective Domain

The affective domain consists of those procedures which attempt to
establish empathetic and harmonious relationships between two individuals,
thus enabling them to communicate without feelings of defensiveness.

Catharsis Procedures

Catharsis procedures include the endeavors of either conference
participant to verbalize his emotions, motivations, feelings, and thoughts
related to problems under discussion. Catharsis involves the "talking
out" of subjective feelings as a means of clearing the air and enabling
one participant to share and comprehend the feelings expressed by the
other.

<u>Example</u>

ST I'm nervous and I have real difficulty in speaking
    with children just sort of on the spur of the moment,
    because I don't speak simply enough. My words are
    much above their comprehension and then I get halfway
    into something and I'm using complicated words and so
    I see blank looks so I go back and start again, but

by that time they already know what's happening. They wonder who is this person or at least I feel this.

Rapport Building Procedures

Rapport building procedures comprise supportive statements by college supervisors which afford confidence and security for teachers. Rapport building includes showing interest in the teachers' problems, stressing the accomplishment of desired objectives, and providing verbal encouragement such as "good," "mm-hm," and "yes, go on."

Example

CS You know, when I read the typescript, I had the same feeling as Mrs. _____ that these children really had responded and they had actually stayed with the discussion.

Social Amenities Procedures

Social amenities procedures imply polite formalities such as friendly conversations, greetings, and socializing.

Example

CS Are you going to bring your lunch?

ST Yes.

CS I'll bring mine. Mrs. _____ brings hers.

Structuring Domain

The structuring domain is composed of routine and directing processes which determine the degree of organization and the tenor of a conference. Included are those procedures which deal with role, topic, time, and space limitations.

Routine Processes

Routine processes provide a basic framework which makes it possible for conferences to proceed in an orderly manner.

Administrative procedures. Administrative procedures focus on the development of policy concerning role expectations. Also included are establishing standards, scheduling, and attending to physical arrangements.

Example

ST Are we going to be put in different seminars next semester?

CS Probably.

ST But you'll still be my advisor, won't you?

CS Uh, do I gather that you wish I could be?

ST Yes, certainly. You're used to me. I'll have to break somebody else in.

Summary procedures. Summary procedures involve recapitulations of major points made during problem solving episodes through conferences as well as remarks which indicate a termination of the conference.

Example

CS You said you felt that you really reached these kids in this lesson. Can you recapitulate for a minute and think what you did that was effective with these kids in this particular lesson?

ST Well, they were interested in the approach that I used to the vocabulary. They liked looking at the pictures and they liked knowing that they had figured out the right answer to what I was looking for, a giraffe, from the picture. They liked knowing that they were able to do that.

Directing Processes

Directing processes include leading and controlling procedures which determine the tenor of the conference and channel communication toward certain ends.

Leading procedures. Leading procedures imply attempts by either
conference participant to persuade or encourage the other to choose topics
for discussion and reach decisions concerning the solution of chosen
topics. Leading statements include initiating and probing areas for
discussion.

Example

CS   Well, to get into this, you made a comment at the end
     of the lesson that I thought was a very good one for
     us to perhaps start off on. You said, "Gee, it went
     pretty good today. They really understood what I was
     talking about."

ST   Yes.

CS   Now I'm wondering if we can find some specific places
     where you thought it was going good and let's see if
     we can figure out why it was going good because I
     thought the same thing.

Controlling procedures. Controlling procedures include attempts
to direct teacher behavior in a forceful manner through regulatory statements such as applying sanctions, reprimanding, and taking corrective
action.

Example

CS   Yes, that was because the noise level was a little
     high. I had the feeling they were perhaps getting
     a little bit restless at this point and maybe push-
     ing to a little faster conclusion or simply request-
     ing a little more quietude and attention earlier
     might have been in order. The noise level, I think,
     was a little high. It was higher there because that's
     where you had to tell them you couldn't hear what was
     going on. I believe that I would have been a little
     more direct right there.

Promissory Model

The final phase in the development of the promissory model consisted of incorporating the postulated system of categories into a schematic representation which illustrates the interrelationships among the category procedures, processes, and domains. In the model, Figure 1, intersecting circles "A," "B," and "C" represent the category domains problem solving, affective, and structuring. Interrelationships among the three category domains are indicated by intersections "AB," "BC," "AC," and "ABC." These interactions transpire in a universe, designated by the letter "U," which is defined as the verbal interaction in supervisory conferences.

Intersection "AB" proposes interrelationships between elements of the problem solving domain and elements of the affective domain. A supervisor's comment, "I don't think you should be greatly surprised or upset about the fact that there is a lot of recall in this lesson; this is in terms of your purpose," may be described in terms of interpreting-evaluating procedures from the problem solving domain and rapport building procedures from the affective domain.

Intersection "BC" proposes interrelationships between elements of the affective and structuring domains. A college supervisor's observation, "I think that your purpose was very good. Let's try and decide how you might do this next time," may be described in terms of rapport building procedures from the affective domain and leading procedures in the structuring domain.

Intersection "AC" suggests connections between elements of the

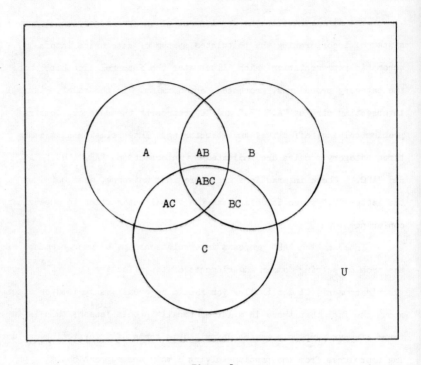

Figure 1

Model for Analyzing and Describing Verbal Interaction
During Supervisory Conferences*

*A = problem solving domain; B = affective domain; C = structuring
domain; AB = intersection of problem solving and affective domains; BC =
intersection of affective and structuring domains; AC = intersection of
problem solving and structuring domains; ABC = intersection of problem
solving, affective, and structuring domains; U = verbal interaction during
supervisory conferences.

problem solving domain and elements of the structuring domain. The supervisor's comment, "Can you recapitulate for a minute and think what you did that was effective with these kids in this particular lesson?" may be described in terms of identifying procedures from the problem solving domain and leading procedures from the structuring domain.

Intersection "ABC" implies interrelationships among all three category domains. A supervisor's observation, "Now I'm wondering if we can find some specific places where you thought it was going good and let's see if you can figure out why it was going good because I thought the same thing," may be described in terms of identifying procedures from the problem solving domain, rapport building procedures from the affective domain, and leading procedures from the structuring domain.

Application and Verifi-
cation of the Model

As a first step in testing the feasibility of the promissory model, units of analysis and coding procedures were identified and defined. A test of reliability was made as a means of providing a quantitative measure of the feasibility.

Units of analysis. In order to test the feasibility of the model, it was necessary to select units of analysis appropriate for analyzing typescripts of supervisory conferences. Medley and Mitzel[1] propose that either a natural or time-unit may be used to measure some behavior or

_____

[1]Donald M. Medley and Harold E. Mitzel, "Measuring Classroom Behavior by Systematic Observation," Handbook of Research on Teaching: A Project of the American Educational Research Association, N. L. Gage, editor (Chicago: Rand McNally and Company, 1963), p. 300.

aspect of behavior. Because typescripts reflect a series of individual verbal behaviors, two natural units of analysis were selected: utterance units and thought units.

An utterance unit is defined as the uninterrupted verbal behavior of either participant in a supervisory conference. Utterance units may consist of one or more thought units. Two examples of utterance units appear below:

Examples

CS   Now, let's see what you might have done to remove that difficulty because this was one that I saw. Those who were at the table changing money were actively involved and did see, but thirty-one others were not actively involved and couldn't see. Taking it from that point, can you see one different course or some other different courses you might have followed?

CS   You want to say something to provoke a reaction, a strong reaction. What if only one youngster responds and says, "I don't agree with that," or "I agree with that"?

For purposes of in-depth analysis of either conference partici-pant's verbal behavior, an utterance unit may be subdivided into its constituent thought units. A thought unit is a statement(s) which expesses a complete idea and represents a shift in the speaker's verbal behavior from one category process and/or procedure to another category process and/or procedures with and among category domains.

The following are examples of the preceding two utterance units subdivided into constituent thought units:

Examples

CS   Now, let's see what you might have done to remove that difficulty because this was one that I saw.// Those who were at the table changing money were actively involved and did see, but thirty-one others were not

actively involved and couldn't see.// Taking it from
that point, can you see one different course or some
other different courses you might have followed?//

CS You want to say something to provoke a reaction, a
strong reaction.// What if only one youngster
responds and says, "I don't agree with that," or
"I agree with that"?//

Coding procedures. Utilizing utterance and/or thought units it is
possible to analyze and describe the verbal interaction of conference
participants in terms of the promissory model. In every instance, coding
is from the coder's viewpoint with meanings inferred from the verbal
behavior of the conference participants. The method of coding is a
modified outline form in which capital letters designate the category
domains, arabic numerals represent the category processes in the problem
solving and structuring domains and the category procedures in the affective
domain, and small letters designate the category procedures in the problem
solving and structuring domains.

After incorporating the coding symbols the system of categories
utilized in coding typescripts appeared as follows:

A. PROBLEM SOLVING DOMAIN

    1. Comprehending processes

        a. Identifying procedures
        b. Defining procedures

    2. Analyzing processes

        a. Interpreting-evaluating procedures
        b. Hypothesizing procedures

B. AFFECTIVE DOMAIN

    1. Catharsis procedures

    2. Rapport building procedures

    3. Social amenities procedures

C. STRUCTURING DOMAIN

    1. Routine processes

        a. Administrative procedures
        b. Summary procedures

    2. Directing processes

        a. Leading procedures
        b. Controlling procedures

D. NON-CODABLE[1]

Two strategies for coding utterance and thought units, unidimensional and multidimensional, were developed. When coding utterance and thought units utilizing the unidimensional method, the coder first infers intent and then codes the unit using only one category process and/or procedure from one of the category domains. The following are examples of coding utterance and thought units using the unidimensional method:

Example of Unidimensional Coding of Utterance Unit

CS You said you felt that you really reached these kids in this lesson. Can you recapitulate for a minute and think what you did that was effective with these kids in this particular lesson? (C-1-b)

Example of Unidimensional Coding of Thought Units

CS I think that your purpose was very good.// (B-2)
     Let's try and decide how you might do this next time.//
     (C-2-a)

When utilizing the multidimensional method to code utterance and thought units, the coder first infers intent and then codes the unit using

---

[1]The coding of typescripts necessitated an additional category "Non-codable." Non-codable statements are those for which no meaning can be inferred because the wording or intent is obscure.

one category process and/or procedure from two or more of the category
domains. No more than one category process and/or procedure may be
assigned from one category domain. The following are examples of coding
utterance and thought units using the multidimensional method:

Example of Multidimensional
Coding of Utterance Unit

CS You knew what concepts you were interested in
beginning with and you had an idea of how you
were going to proceed and you also had an idea
how you were going to evaluate this lesson.
(A-2-a; C-1-b)

Example of Multidimensional
Coding of Thought Units

CS I think you've just mentioned quite a few things we
were thinking of as you prepared for this lesson,
especially with respect to the new vocabulary, and
that section appealed to me too.// (A-2-a; B-2;
C-2-a) Can we go back for a minute again and just
think of what specific things you had in mind when
you worked?// (A-1-a; C-2-a)

Berelson has suggested that large units of analysis generally
provide as accurate a profile of content as small units.[1] Therefore,
coding utterance units with either the unidimensional or the multidimensional method should provide an effective procedure for gross
analysis of supervisor's verbal teaching behavior. Coding thought units
with either method would provide a more detailed analysis.

Test of reliability. In order to provide a quantitative measure
of the feasibility of the model a test of reliability was conducted by
independently coding 270 utterance units using the multidimensional coding

---

[1]Bernard Berelson, Content Analysis in Communication Research
(Glencoe, Illinois: The Free Press, 1952).

method. The 270 utterance units were assembled by arbitrarily choosing fifteen consecutive utterance units from each of eighteen typescripts. The eighteen typescripts represented one conference between each of six college supervisors and their three student teachers.

After all units had been independently coded, the codings were compared and the percentage of agreement between the coders was computed. The overall coding reliability was 92.8 percent and the range was from 79.3 to 100.0 percent for the multidimensional coding of the 270 utterance units in the sample.

Conclusions and Recommendations

The methodology employed in this study appears to be a justifiable means for developing a category system to analyze and describe the verbal interaction between college supervisors and student teachers. The first two phases of rational reconstruction were useful in developing a promissory model. Critical areas of the study were identifying the literature to be analyzed, specifying the unit of analysis, developing categories for analysis, and stipulating criteria to organize the dimensions of performance into categories and categories into a category system.

Behavioral illustrations, selected from actual conference typescripts, were stipulated for each procedural definition in the category system. Since these behavioral instances are observable in reality, it is concluded that the proposed category procedures are valid.

The practicality of the model was tested by analyzing 270 utterance units selected from eighteen typescripts of supervisory conferences. An overall reliability of 92.8 percent was obtained, indicating that the

promissory model can be a useful instrument for describing verbal interaction in individualized conferences between student teachers and college
supervisors.

The variables of a supervisory conference are tentatively identified
by the category system. These should aid future researchers to generate
hypotheses regarding the relationships between the verbal interaction of
supervisors and student teachers in supervisory conferences and the subsequent verbal interaction between student teachers and pupils during
teaching sessions.

It is recommended that the feasibility of the model be tested more
extensively using various approaches to supervisory conferences, including
conferences between cooperating teachers and student teachers. The
reliability of the model itself needs more intensive testing.

No attempt was made to identify the possible interrelationships
among the category domains. Through plotting the various patterns of
interactions identified in typescripts, researchers may be able to
postulate the roles of supervisors and student teachers during conferences.
It may be possible to stipulate effective patterns of verbal teaching
behavior for college supervisors and to test these patterns through the
response of student teachers to them.

A promissory model can be useful in the preparation of college
supervisors in making them aware of their teaching behavior and aiding
them in analyzing it objectively.

Variations in conference styles suggest an interesting possibility
for analysis. Perhaps different conference styles can be described in terms
of patterns of verbal teaching behavior on the part of college supervisors.

THE PROMISSORY MODEL--A SYSTEM OF CATEGORIES FOR ANALYZING
VERBAL INTERACTION IN SUPERVISORY CONFERENCES

Problem Solving Domain

Comprehending processes

> Identifying procedures
> Defining procedures

Analyzing processes

> Interpreting-evaluating procedures
> Hypothesizing procedures

Affective Domain

> Catharsis procedures
> Rapport building procedures
> Social amenities procedures

Structuring Domain

Routine processes

> Administrative procedures
> Summary procedures

Directing processes

> Leading procedures
> Controlling procedures

Chapter V

THE COOPERATING TEACHER AS TEACHING TUTOR[1]
Ruth Heidelbach

Cooperating teachers assume one of the most significant roles in
the professional education laboratory. These individuals are considered
master teachers in the classroom as well as supervisors of students of
teaching. The dual focus of their teaching responsibilities places them
in many and varied instructional situations. The study that is reported
in this chapter deals with a systematic investigation into one aspect of
their teaching as it relates to supervision of student teachers. It
focuses on the supervisory conference, a dyadic situation which can be
thought of as tutorial. As a teaching tutor the cooperating teacher
engages in individualized instruction.

Background and Purpose of This Study

The purpose of this study was to develop a tentative model for
analyzing and describing the verbal behavior of cooperating teachers

---

[1]Ruth Ann Heidelbach, "The Development of a Tentative Model for
Analyzing and Describing the Verbal Behavior of Cooperating Teachers in
Conference with Student Teachers" (unpublished Ed.D. report, Teachers
College, Columbia University, 1967).

engaged in individualized teaching in conferences with student teachers.
The tentative model was compared with a "Promissory Model" developed by
Brown-Hoffman for analyzing the verbal interaction between college
supervisors and student teachers during supervisory conferences.[1]

That cooperating teachers have important influence on student
teachers is unquestionable.

> The supervising teacher is seen by students, and
> increasingly by the Teacher Educator, as the most important
> single influence on the student teacher.[2]

> Cooperating teachers hold a significant and enviable
> position among teacher educators. Studies of beginning
> teachers, follow-up studies of graduates from teacher
> education programs, and students' evaluation of their
> college preparation reveal that student teaching and
> other laboratory experiences have profound influence
> in determining the kind of teacher the student becomes.[3]

> It is quite evident that the nature and extent of
> the contact the student teacher has with his supervising
> (cooperating) teacher provide the setting for the "posi-
> tive impact." . . . Student teachers will both consciously
> and unconsciously absorb the standards and ideas of the
> supervising teacher. If this impact is to be a positive
> one, the need for quality in supervision must be emphasized.[4]

If indeed the cooperating teacher is an important influence, studies which

---

[1]See Chapter IV.

[2]Bernard Rabin, "Who Are the Supervising Teachers?" The Supervising
Teacher, Thirty-seventh Yearbook of the Association for Student Teaching
(Cedar Falls, Iowa: The Association, 1959), p. 2.

[3]Florence B. Stratemeyer and Margaret Lindsey, Working with
Student Teachers (New York: Bureau of Publications, Teachers College,
Columbia University, 1958), p. 4.

[4]Robert B. Hayes, "Involving Teachers in Teacher Education,"
Professional Growth Inservice of the Supervising Teacher, Forty-fifth
Yearbook of the Association for Student Teaching (Cedar Falls, Iowa:
The Association, 1966), p. 4.

lead teacher educators to understand more fully the influences of cooperating teachers would seem to be useful. Teacher educators, both preservice and in-service, are faced with the task of preparing vast numbers of cooperating teachers in new and effective ways without the advantage of research findings to help in decision-making.

The writers of New Horizons for the Teaching Profession call attention to the need for colleges to organize programs in which the work of the cooperating teacher can be studied.[1] One focus for studying the work of the cooperating teacher is described by Taba.

> Under the twin impact of continued criticism of education and an increased flow of money into research and experimentation, a new interest has been kindled in the theory of instruction and the analysis of the teaching act. Conviction is growing that to understand either, we must study teaching as it occurs in the classroom instead of inferring its effectiveness from the personality characteristics of teachers, or from a general list of a priori competencies. . . . In this shift of focus of studying teaching and learning in the classroom the emphasis is on interaction. The description of teaching acts becomes the chief tool for securing information.[2]

In discussing the status of teacher education, Smith and Meux have the following to say about the teaching acts to which Taba alludes in her proposal for gathering information related to the effectiveness of teaching:

---

[1]Margaret Lindsey (ed.), New Horizons for the Teaching Profession, A Report of the Task Force on New Horizons in Teacher Education and Professional Standards (Washington, D.C.: National Education Association, 1961).

[2]Hilda Taba, Samuel Levine and Freeman F. Elzey, Thinking in Elementary School Children, U.S. Office of Education Cooperative Research Project, No. 1574 (San Francisco: San Francisco State College, 1964), p. 44.

The instructional system is a system of factors. By a system is here meant that the factors are related to one another, that they inter-act, and that together they constitute a unit which can be analyzed and studied empirically to determine the regularities that hold within it. These regularities will obtain for the class of all instructional situations, but there may be sub-classes (italics not in the original) in which additional regularities may be found. Furthermore, it should be noted that the instructional situation can be studied quite apart from treatments and their administration. In fact it may well be that the failure to obtain consistent results from comparative studies of treatment is due in part to the fact that the instructional situation has not been studied on its own account and hence regularities that affect treatments have not been recognized.[1]

Cooperating teachers' conferences are viewed as a fruitful area for study to determine the "factors" which exist in the interaction of cooperating teachers and student teachers. The focus for this study was seen as a possible "sub-class" referred to by Smith and Meux. As these investigators suggest, this study attempted to examine instruction (individualized teaching by cooperating teachers) "quite apart from treatments and their administration."

Gage discusses the need for the development of a theory of teaching and has the following to say about the need for such investigation:

Teachers must know how to manipulate the independent variables, especially their own behaviors, that determine learning. Such knowledge cannot be derived automatically from knowledge about the learning process. To explain the control the teaching act requires a science and technology of teaching in its own right. The student of educational psychology who complains that he has learned much about the learning process and learners,

---

[1]B. Othanel Smith and Milton Meux, "Research in Teacher Education: Problems and Criticism," An Analysis and Projection of Research in Teacher Education, by Frederick R. Cyphert and Ernest Spaights (Columbus, Ohio: The Ohio State University Research Foundation, 1964), p. 114.

but not about teaching, is asking for the fruits of scientific inquiry, including theories of teaching.[1]

For cooperating teachers to understand and control their verbal teaching behavior in conferences they will need knowledge about and conceptions of teaching. They cannot fully conceptualize teaching solely from knowledge about the learning processes and learners with whom they are participating in the supervisory conference.

In formulating a scientifically-oriented theory of teaching in supervisory conferences with student teachers, as suggested by Gage, reference is made to Nagel, who defined the nature of knowledge in the scientific sense.

> It is the desire for explanations which are at once systematic and controllable by factual evidence that generates science; and it is the organization and classi-fication of knowledge on the basis of explanatory princi-ples that is the distinctive goal of the sciences. . . . Science seeks to discover and formulate in general terms the condition under which events of various sorts occur. . . . This goal can be achieved only by distinguishing or isolating certain properties in the subject matter being studied and by ascertaining the reliable patterns of dependence in which these properties stand to one another.[2]

Nagel calls for verification, identification, classification of variables and establishment of relationships between these variables based on explanatory principles identified in certain phenomena. Nagel's explanation of scientifically-established knowledge is seen here as the "fruits of scientific inquiry, including theories of teaching" referred

---

[1]N. L. Gage, "Theories of Teaching," Theories of Learning and Instruction, Sixty-third Yearbook of the National Society for the Study of Education, Part I (Chicago: The University Press, 1964), p. 273.

[2]Ernest Nagel, The Structure of Science (New York: Harcourt, Brace, and World, 1961), p. 4.

to by Gage.

Cyphert and Spaights refer to the lack of "empirically-verified data" in teacher education as they describe the present basis for decision-making aimed at improvement of teacher education programs.

> When one pursues the change made in teacher education over the past ten years, or projects ahead for the next decade, he is struck with the undeniable evidence that virtually all of those who are planning the "improvement" of teacher education are operating, and are likely to continue to operate, by applying their own subjective insight, hunches and hypotheses growing out of experience to reorganize portions of their programs. They have neither pre- nor post-innovational empirical data concerning the validity of their changes. The fact that most efforts to improve the preparation of teachers are superficial in research context, and that new knowledge is ignored or missing altogether, makes little sense in light of widespread dissatisfaction with the state of the art. Too long too many teacher educators have enjoyed the comfort of opinion without the discomfort of evidence.[1]

These observations support the idea that teacher education lacks a grand conceptual scheme which can be used to predict and control decisions. Teacher educators are at a point when they must begin to establish verified knowledge which can be used to predict the consequences of decisions which they make.

Merton defines theory as "logically interconnected conceptions which are limited and modest in scope rather than all embracing and grandiose." Merton's position on developing needed theories in the emerging field of sociology is explained in the following quotation from his writing. He defines "Theories of the Middle Range."

---

[1]Frederick R. Cyphert and Ernest Spaights, An Analysis and Projection of Research in Teacher Education, Cooperative Research Project No. F-15 (Columbus, Ohio: The Ohio State University Research Foundation, 1964), p. 2.

> Theories of the Middle Range: theories intermediate
> to the minor working hypotheses evolved in abundance
> during day-by-day routines of research, and the all-
> inclusive speculations comprising a master conceptual
> scheme from which it is hoped to derive a very large
> number of empirically observed uniformities of social
> behavior.[1]

It is the position which Merton has taken that gives the basic rationale

for this investigation as it relates to the development of theories in

teacher education. The development of control, understanding, and

prediction of teaching in supervisory conferences with student teachers

was seen as a contribution to a theory of the middle range in teacher

education.

The development of a model for analyzing and describing the verbal

behavior of cooperating teachers in conference with student teachers is a

basic step in the processes of establishing a theory of supervisory con-

ferences. The development of such a model was the purpose of this study.

Focus of the Study

The phenomena observed and investigated in the initial phase were

the individualized verbal teaching behaviors of cooperating teachers in

supervisory conferences with student teachers. A cooperating teacher's

supervisory conference has been described by Stratemeyer and Lindsey.

> The conference is a means of communication involving
> two or more persons for the purpose of serious conversation
> or discussion. It is communication for the purpose of
> counseling or advising, for pooling the results of each
> individual's best thinking, for considering together a

---

[1]Robert K. Merton, Social Theory and Social Structure (rev. ed.;
Glencoe, Ill.: The Free Press, 1957), p. 5.

common interest or concern. In essence, the conference in the professional education of teachers is a teacher-learning situation (italics not in the original); it is a meeting of the minds with mutual concern for the best interests of children or youth and of the individuals involved in the conference.[1]

Although supervisory conferences sometimes take place between more than two participants, the focus of this investigation was the dyadic situation involving one cooperating teacher and one student teacher.

Individualized teaching has been described by DeHaan and Doll:

1. In individualized teaching the emphasis is on the pupil as a person, the teacher as a person, and the interaction which takes place between them. In such an interpersonal relationship, the pupil can face the world and accept himself in a way which facilitates release of potential. (Italics not in original.)

2. Individualization occurs when a teacher recognizes and responds to the emotional reactions of the learner as well as to his academic achievement, his intellectual mistake, or his mental deficiencies, i.e., when the teacher responds to the pupil as a whole person and not just as a learner of subject matter.

3. Individualization occurs when the teacher goes beyond ordinary achievement. . . . A teacher makes achievement . . . a means to an end of motivating the pupil to further learning.

4. Individualization also occurs when the teacher considers the pupil to be an individual with unique perceptions, values, concepts and needs, and when he creatively fashions learning opportunities to enhance the pupil's individuality.

5. Individualization is meant to lead to commitment and purposes, to sensitivity to others' needs, to awareness

---

[1] Florence Stratemeyer and Margaret Lindsey, Working with Student Teachers (New York: Bureau of Publications, Teachers College, Columbia University, 1958), p. 396.

to the demands of truth and justice.[1]

Emphasis on the student, interaction, and release of the student's potential as a teacher are problems of serious concern to both participants in a supervisory conference. The participants are involved in discourse which touches on the total range of the phenomena dealt with by the teacher in his daily experiences.

The student teacher and the cooperating teacher deal with this substance not solely for the purpose of gaining control over the immediate situation. The student does not attempt to "practice" what his cooperating teacher does, but rather he goes beyond the implications of the classroom in which he is learning to become a teacher. He and his cooperating teacher build toward conceptions of teaching behavior as they relate to the uniqueness of the student as a person and to his professional potential.

Combs suggests that today the professional dealing with human problems regards himself as an "intelligent human being using himself, his knowledge, and the resources at hand to solve the problems for which he is responsible."[2]

> If we adopt this "self as instrument" concept of the professional worker to teaching, it means that teacher-education programs must concern themselves with persons, not competencies. It means that the individualization of instruction we have sought for the public schools must be applied to these programs as well. It calls for the shifting and changing to meet the demands and opportunities

---

[1] Robert F. DeHaan and Ronald C. Doll, "Individualization and Human Potential," Individualizing Instruction, Yearbook of the Association for Supervision and Curriculum Development (Washington, D.C.: The Association, 1964), pp. 19-20.

[2] Arthur W. Combs, The Professional Education of Teachers (Boston: Allyn and Bacon, Inc., 1965), p. 8.

afforded in daily tasks. Such a teacher will not behave in a set way. (Italics not in the original.) His behavior will change from moment to moment, from day to day, adjusting continually and smoothly to the needs of his students, the situation he is in, the purposes he seeks to fulfill, and the methods and materials at his command.

The good teacher is no carbon copy but possesses something intensely his own. Artists sometimes call this "the discovery of one's own personal idiom."[1]

If the cooperating teacher endeavors to use his verbal behavior "as an instrument" for the purpose of helping the student "discover his own personal idiom," then he will be considering the "uniqueness" referred to by DeHaan and Doll.

"Commitment, purposes, and sensitivity to others," mentioned by DeHaan and Doll, and "concern for the best interest of children and youth," referred to by Stratemeyer and Lindsey describe the direction of changes in the behavior of the teacher as he adjusts continually to the needs of the students, the situations, purposes, methods, and materials. Combs sees these changes as the teacher using himself as an instrument.

One means of communication in a conference is through verbal behavior of the participants. Verbal behavior is used here, as it has been used in much of the current research on teaching, to mean the vocalized languages used to communicate meaning in the teaching-learning situation. Verbal dimensions of the conference make up one means of dyadic communication discussed by Stratemeyer and Lindsey. Verbal behavior in the conference is one aspect of cooperating teachers' individualized teaching. Verbal behavior is one type of supervisory or tutorial teaching behavior.

---

[1]Ibid., p. 9.

118

Development of a Tentative Model

Discussion of the procedures in developing the tentative model for describing the verbal interaction between cooperating teachers and student teachers during their conferences requires the use of terminology that needs clarification at the outset. Following are the definitions of such terms:

Model: Categories of verbal behavior of cooperating teachers in conference with student teachers and procedures for using the categories.

Category: A classificatory name given to a group of verbal behaviors of cooperating teachers in conference with student teachers.

Learning behaviors: The full range of behaviors on the part of any learner that are directly related to teaching behaviors described above.

Verbal teaching behavior: Verbal utterances made by teachers or students in response to verbal utterances by either individual.

Cooperating teacher: An individual designated by the college and the school to accept responsibility of inducting a student into the professional activities of a teacher through direct experiences in the school, classroom, and community.

Individualized teaching: Tutorial teaching that takes place in the dyadic situation--a cooperating teacher and student teacher conference.

Conference: A designated time for discussion by the cooperating teacher and the student teacher of the concerns, problems, interests, and actions of either participant.

Student teachers: Individuals who are participating in direct experiences in the schools, under the guidance of a cooperating teacher in whose classroom they take increasing responsibility for the work with a group of pupils.

Nature and Source of the Data

The data used in the formulation of the categories which are part
of the tentative model were typescripts of taped conferences with student
teachers held by six cooperating teachers. At the time of the study the
teachers were licensed public elementary school teachers. The range of
teaching experience in the group of teachers was from four to ten years.
Most had taught three or four years in the school in which the study took
place. Only one teacher had taught in another school system. Grades one,
three, five, and six of the elementary school were represented in the data.
The teachers were all experienced cooperating teachers, having had at
least two years' experience with student teachers. All attended colleges
and universities in the metropolitan area in which the elementary school
was located.

Each teacher recorded three conferences over a period of five weeks.
Student teachers had taught lessons in various subjects which are normally
thought of as comprising the curriculum of the elementary school. The
conferences were held at a time when the cooperating teacher and student
teacher could talk over the student's teaching.

Student teachers working with the cooperating teachers were
participating in a preservice program during their first semester student
teaching experience. Recent graduates of liberal arts colleges, their
ages ranged from twenty to twenty-six years. Their baccalaureate degrees
were in different areas of specialization. Only one student had had no
experience prior to entering the fifth year program in childhood education.

Categories comprising the Promissory Model developed by Brown-
Hoffman used in the comparative phase of this study appear in Chapter IV.

120

Three major Domains of supervisory verbal behavior are indicated, each with subcategories, referred to as Procedures and/or Processes.

Treatment of the Data

As with much of the research on teaching that preceded this study, data treatment involved the application of content analysis. Berelson reviewed the distinguishing characteristics of content analysis and offers the following definition: "Content analysis is a research technique for the objective, systematic, and quantitative description of the manifest content of communication."[1]

Three phases of data treatment made up the "objective systematic description" of the individualized verbal teaching behavior of cooperating teachers in conference with student teachers.

Phase One: Initial Analysis of the Data,
Using Classificatory Principles

Tentative categories were established as described by Selltiz et al.

> In working with unstructured evidence (typescripts of tape recordings), . . . the first problem is to arrive at decisions about which aspects of the material are to be categorized—that is, what classificatory principles are to be used in establishing sets of categories.[2]

Establishment of categories from classificatory principles followed the steps outlined by these authors. They suggest that because of the nature of exploratory investigations, an investigator does not begin classifying

---

[1]Bernard Berelson, Content Analysis in Communication Research (Glencoe, Ill.: The Free Press, 1952), p. 18.

[2]Claire Selltiz et al., Research Methods in Social Relations (2 vols.: New York: Dryden Press, 1951), p. 399.

data with explicit hypotheses which will yield classificatory principles. Since there have not been studies dealing with the identification of the dimensions of the verbal behavior of cooperating teachers in conference with student teachers, this investigator considered the present study exploratory in relation to the nature of the phenomena under investigation

Rules for classification set forth by Kerlinger were used in formulating classificatory principles.[1] They are:

1. Categories are set up according to the research problem and purpose.
2. The categories are exhaustive.
3. The categories are mutually exclusive and independent.
4. Each category (variable) is derived from one classification principle.
5. Any categorization scheme must be on one level of discourse.

An explanation of the use of these rules follows in the description of the phases of the data treatment.

First classification of the data—establishing indicators of function and content. From eighteen typescripts of cooperating teachers' conferences, nine were systematically selected for use in the formulation of the tentative model. During the initial analysis the investigator read these nine typescripts. Similar groups of verbal behavior were identified and recorded. Kerlinger's first rule of categorization was used here in formulating the first classificatory principle. Cooperating teacher verbal behavior would be classified by identifying the function and content of the verbal behavior in the conferences. Since the purpose of the research problem was to describe and analyze verbal behavior, it

---

[1]Fred N. Kerlinger, Foundations of Behavioral Research (New York: Holt, Rinehart, and Winston, 1965), p. 606.

was thought that categories that identify function and content of verbal behavior would be relevant. In the initial analysis of the data <u>121 indicators of the function and substance (content) of the verbal behavior were identified</u>.

<u>Second classification of the data—establishing exhaustive indicators</u>. Kerlinger's second rule for categorization was used to refine the universe of indicators identified in the first classification. The second classificatory principle used states that <u>all indicators of one function of verbal behavior would be categorized as a single indicator and that all substantive talk (content) would be categorized as a single indicator</u>.

<u>Functional indicators</u> identified in this step were as follows: referring, asking, re-stating, describing, explaining, clarifying, reacting, agreeing or disagreeing, assuming, anticipating, summarizing, and prescribing. <u>Substantive indicators</u> identified were: student teacher teaching behavior, cooperating teacher teaching behavior, generalized teaching behavior, characteristics of children, instructional materials, the conference, special teachers, and verbal behavior of the student teacher.

<u>Third classification of the data—establishing mutually exclusive categories derived from one classificatory principle</u>. The principle used during the third classification stated that the <u>indicators identified in the previous categorization would be analyzed and classified into mutually exclusive and independent categories. Each category would be derived from one classification principle</u>. This principle was derived using Kerlinger's third and fourth rules.

Three principles of classification were adapted from Stratemeyer and Lindsey's definition of the purpose of a supervisory conference. These purposes were: (1) "to counsel and advise, (2) to pool ideas and thinking, and (3) to consider common interests and concerns."[1]

Counseling and advising functions were classified into a mutually exclusive category referred to as Prescriptive Operations, verbal behavior of a cooperating teacher that function as a prescription for a teaching behavior. These Operations included indicators associated with Prescriptions of teaching behaviors such as: thinking or guessing, considering a proposal, making a proposition, implying something directly or indirectly expressed, assuming, anticipating, or hypothesizing or generalizing.

Pooling ideas and thinking functions were classified into a mutually exclusive category referred to as Descriptive Operations and included the following indicators of cooperating teacher verbal behavior: describing, restating, clarifying, explaining, summarizing, agreeing, and disagreeing. In Descriptive Operations, the cooperating teachers were attempting to order the phenomena related to the content or substance of the verbal behavior.

Common interests and concerns of the cooperating teacher and the student teacher found in the data were classified as a mutually exhaustive category referred to as Substantive Areas. Substantive Areas include the content or problems that form the core or nucleus of a unit of verbal

---

[1]Florence B. Stratemeyer and Margaret Lindsey, Working with Student Teachers (New York: Bureau of Publications, Teachers College, Columbia University, 1958), p. 396.

behavior. These areas can be thought of as problems that form the content of the student teaching experience.

One further classification of the data was needed. Verbal behavior that functioned as an indicator of the substance of the discourse was classified into a mutually exclusive category referred to as Focusing Operations. Focusing Operations include the following indicators of cooperating teacher verbal behavior: referring and asking.

The initial analysis of the data using classificatory principles resulted in the formulation of four major categories of cooperating teacher verbal behavior. They are: Focusing Operations, Descriptive Operations, Prescriptive Operations, and Substantive Areas.

Phase Two: Testing the Categories for Reliability

During phase two the categories were tested for reliability. Ten impartial judges were asked to subject the categories to a series of dichotomous decisions as developed by Schutz.[1] Following this procedure the investigator established for each category a dichotomous category. For example, in the analysis of the typescripts the investigator established as one category indicator of verbal behavior described as "ask a question." A dichotomous condition related to this dimension of behavior might be "tell an answer." The judges were presented with systematically selected sections of the data upon which they were to base their decisions as to whether the cooperating teacher was "asking" or "telling."

---

[1]William C. Schutz, "On Categorizing Qualitative Data in Content Analysis," Public Opinion Quarterly, 22:502-515, Winter, 1958.

Schutz developed tables of agreement that were used to describe
the levels of agreement reached in the decisions made by the judges in the
reliability test. Schutz suggests that judgments should reach at least
the .80, .85, or .95 level of agreement.[1] The results of the test for
reliability of the tentative categories describing the verbal behavior of
cooperating teachers indicated that all categories could be considered
reliable at one of the suggested levels of agreement.

Phase Three: Establishing the Reliability of the Coding Procedures and Analysis of the Remaining Data

Phase three consisted of the analysis of the remaining nine typescripts using the established Operational and Substantive Categories.
Units of analysis consisted of sentences or groups of sentences that
could be coded as one Operational Category of verbal behavior and the
Substantive Area(s) that was (were) the focus of the Operational discourse.
This unit of analysis is found within a larger unit of verbal behavior
defined as uninterrupted talk of the cooperating teacher.

Reliability of the coding procedures was established using two competent judges as analysts. Results of the judgments for establishing the
reliability of the coding procedures indicated that the range of agreement
for the nine conferences was from 60 to 100 percent. The average agreement for all nine conferences was 84 percent.

During the coding analysts identified nine new Substantive Areas.
They were: The Curriculum, School Routines, Parents and Family,

---

[1]William C. Schutz, "Reliability, Ambiguity, and Content Analysis,"
Psychological Review, 59:125-126, March, 1952.

Administrative/Supervisory Behavior, Other Teacher Behavior, School Nurse,
Plan for Teaching, The Professional Sequence, Community Agencies, and
School Monitor. These areas were added to the Substantive Areas originally
identified by the investigator during the initial analysis of the data.
As a result of these findings the Substantive Areas identified in the data
totaled twenty.

The Tentative Model: Categories and Definitions

Categories and procedures for using the categories form the Tentative Model for analyzing the verbal teaching behavior of cooperating
teachers in conference with student teachers. The following discussion
presents the categories and their definitions. The categories are two-
dimensional: Operational and Substantive.

Operational Verbal Behavior

Operational verbal behavior was classified in three ways which
indicated the nature of its function: focusing, describing, and
prescribing.

Focusing operations indicated verbal behavior that calls
attention to or denotes the substantive area to be discussed.

Referring means to denote, allude to, or initiate.

Asking means to inquire, examine, solicit, invite,
or investigate.

Descriptive operations order the phenomena of the substantive
talk.

Clarifying means to interpret, illuminate, reason,
infer, or imply.

Describing means to define or portray.

<u>Summarizing</u> means to abstract from previous discourse.

<u>Agreeing</u> means to accept a position or point of view.

<u>Restating</u> means to repeat what has been said.

<u>Reacting</u> means to reply in a subjective way.

<u>Prescriptive operations</u> are statements made by the cooperating teacher which prescribe the nature of a teaching behavior that did, will, or might have taken place.

<u>To think or guess</u> the nature of a teaching behavior.

<u>To consider</u> a proposal for a teaching behavior.

<u>To make a proposition</u> for a teaching behavior.

<u>To anticipate or hypothesize</u> a teaching behavior.

<u>To generalize</u> a teaching behavior.

Substantive Verbal Behavior

The second dimension of the categories was the Substantive verbal behavior. A Substantive Area identified what the participants in the conference were talking about. Each Operational verbal behavior was accompanied by at least one Substantive Area. At times a unit of cooperating teacher verbal behavior contained as many as five Substantive Areas.

<u>Student Teacher Teaching Behavior</u>--any teaching behavior which any student teacher did, does, or might perform. The cooperating teacher and the student teacher discuss the student's teaching behavior; make judgments about it; predict how it might be improved; explain pupils' response to it.

<u>Cooperating Teacher Teaching Behavior</u>--any teaching behavior which any cooperating teacher did, does, or might perform. The cooperating teacher uses himself as an example to clarify a point he is attempting to make. He also judges his teaching behavior and makes predictions as to its effectiveness.

<u>Generalized Teaching Behavior</u>--any teaching behavior which any teacher did, does, or might perform. This type of teaching behavior can be thought of as a generalization. The cooperating teacher talks about <u>Generalized Teaching Behavior</u>

when he is making a prescription about appropriate or inappropriate teaching behavior.

Characteristics of Children--a Substantive Area dealing with any description of any child or group of children who have been, are, or will be taught by any teacher. Usually these are children in the class taught by the cooperating teacher, but they can be children in other classes or hypothetical children.

Content--the subject matter which makes up the substance of any lesson taught by any teacher. Usually the content deals with one or more of the areas usually thought of as part of the curriculum of the elementary school.

Instructional Materials--any material which any teacher uses in any teaching behavior which is performed. These materials may be such things as a chalkboard, pictures, tape recorders, notebooks, charts, or texts.

The Conference--actual discussion of any phase of the interaction which takes place between the cooperating teacher and the student teacher during the conference.

The Lesson--a planned or unplanned experience which is provided for a group of children or an individual child. The lesson may have been taught or will be taught. It can be taught by the cooperating teacher, the student, or other teachers. Discussion of the lesson can include discussion of the content of the lesson, materials, children, or teaching behavior.

The Student Teaching Experience--the full range of experiences or part of the experiences which any student has in a classroom, school, and/or community.

Special Teachers--individuals whose teaching responsibilities are other than those of the regular classroom teacher. These individuals may teach music or be associated with the school as liaison people between parents, community, and school. They may teach children, other teachers, or parents.

The Curriculum--the cooperating teacher's discussion of any part of the phenomena usually associated with curriculum as a planned experience. The participants of the conferences refer to both the school curriculum and the curriculum designed by teacher-educators to prepare individuals for teaching responsibilities in the elementary school.

Parents and Family--the discussion of parents, home situation, and siblings in order to bring further meaning to a description of a child. This talk refers to either a description of the home situation or characteristics of individuals within the family.

Administrative/Supervisory Behavior--verbal behavior related to the types of administrative and supervisory behaviors which are discussed by the participants in the conference. These administrators and supervisors are individuals working within the school.

Other Teacher Behavior--discussion of other teachers' teaching behavior. These teachers may be colleagues within the school, but may also be teachers in other schools. These are not special teachers.

Plan for Teaching--any plan which any teacher had made or might make for teaching.

Community Agencies--discussions of the various agencies within the school community which directly influence the lives of the children in the community.

School Monitor--children who assume some responsibility for minor administrative and supervisory routines.

Professional Sequence--references to any aspect of any pre-service student's professional preparation.

The following sample illustrates the application of the categories to supervisory teaching. Code indicators in the margins of the typescript identify the classifications of the verbal teaching behavior. An explanation of the code indicators is presented in Figure 1.

SAMPLE TYPESCRIPT

CT   Well, what did you--your lesson was good. I   FO//SB/LN/CC

      think that they're catching on to the rhymes.

ST   You know, I don't know how you feel about this,

      but sometimes I think some of them are so

      anxious to be the first to answer.

CT   Yes.   DS//CC

ST   They just scream out anything just so they'll

130

	be the first one to answer.	
CT	Yes, like Sylvia.	DS//CC
ST	They don't even think.	
CT	Sylvia.	DS//CC
ST	They, they don't even think what they're saying. They just answer.	
CT	Yes, I think they do.// You have to,	DS//CC
	you know, you have to stop them. You have to	PR//SR/CC
	get them a little more settled. You know,	
	even tell them, "Let's stop before just	
	give out the answer and think about it first."	
	//Raising their hands gives them time	DS//CC//SB
	to think about it, too, you know, so it	
	serves a double purpose.// What I felt was	PR/SB/LN/CC
	that you--when you had them bring their	
	chairs out, I think this almost set a tone	
	that carried through. You know, that was	
	unfortunately carried through the lesson.	

The Tentative Model: Graphic Representations

Graphic representations were seen by this investigator as presentations of variables and their relationships as found in the verbal teaching behavior of cooperating teachers in conference with student teachers. Three models are included: (1) The Smaller Unit of Verbal Behavior; (2) The Sequence of Operational Categories; and (3) The Larger Unit of Verbal Behavior.

Name of Category	Code Indicator
Focusing Operations	FO
Descriptive Operations	DS
Prescriptive Operations	PR
Substantive Categories	
Student Teacher Teaching Behavior	SB
Cooperating Teacher Teaching Behavior	CB
Generalized Teaching Behavior	GB
Characteristics of Children	CC
Content	CN
Instructional Materials	IM
The Conference	CF
The Lesson	LN
The Student Teaching Experience	ST
Special Teachers	SP
Noncodable	NC
Cooperating Teacher	CT
Student Teacher	ST

Figure 1

Tentative Categories and Code Indicators

The Smaller Unit of Verbal Behavior

The Smaller Unit of Verbal Behavior included an Operational
Category and one or more Substantive Areas. Figure 2 presents a model of
this unit. The pattern of variables includes Area O which is an area
representing the Operational Behavior. This area could be a Focusing,
Descriptive, or Prescriptive Operation. Area S represents the Twenty
Substantive Areas which might be found with this Operation. Each box
within this area represents one Substantive Area. In the model presented
in Figure 2 there are five Substantive Areas occurring with the Operational
Behavior. This is indicated by the overlap of Area S on Area O. A model
indicating the presence of one Operation and two Substantive Areas would
appear with Area O overlapped by two boxes in Area S.

The Sequence of Operational
Verbal Behavior

The Sequence of Operational Verbal Behavior included possible
combinations of Operational talk. Operational talk occurred in the data.
Sequences A, B, and C each present six Smaller Units of verbal behavior.
These units include an Operational Category, indicated by Areas F, D, or
P, and Substantive Categories, indicated by the areas with diagonal lines.

Sequence A begins with a Focusing Unit. Some sequences found in
the data began with a Focusing Unit. Not all Focusing was done by the
cooperating teacher; sometimes the student teacher focused the nature of
the substantive talk. When this occurred the first operation in a unit of
cooperating teachers' verbal behavior was coded either as a Focusing,
Descriptive, or Prescriptive Operation.

Following the Focusing Unit in sequence A, the cooperating teacher

133

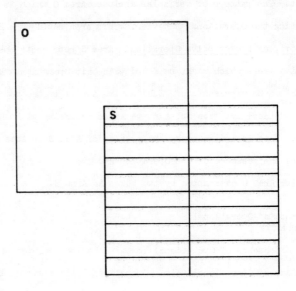

Key

    Area O--Operational Behavior
    Area S--Twenty Substantive Areas

Figure 2

Model of the Smaller Unit of Verbal Behavior

used three Descriptive Units. These were followed by one Prescriptive Unit. The sequence stopped or was interrupted by the student teacher after a Focusing Unit.

Sequence B begins with Describing, continues with a Prescription followed by three Descriptive Units, and ends with a Prescription.

Sequence C begins with a Prescription, followed by Describing, Focusing, Description, Prescription, and stops after a Descriptive Operation.

The sequence of Operational verbal behavior was found to follow no particular pattern or sequence. Sequences began with any of the three Operations. Cooperating teachers ended a series of Smaller Units of Verbal Behavior with Focusing, Descriptive, or Prescriptive talk. Figure 3 presents this model.

The Larger Unit of Verbal Behavior

In analyzing the data, coders were instructed to code Smaller Units of Verbal Behavior within Larger Units of Verbal Behavior. The Larger Unit of Verbal Behavior included uninterrupted talk by the cooperating teacher, and might include any number of smaller units. Uninterrupted talk was preceded by student teacher talk and followed by student teacher talk. If the student interrupted the cooperating teacher before he had completed the thought he was expressing, the unit was considered a completed Larger Unit of Verbal Behavior. Coders could read as much of the data as necessary to make a coding decision.

Figure 4 presents a graphic description of an example of uninterrupted cooperating teacher talk. In this figure the Smaller Unit of Verbal Behavior is represented by a diagonal division indicating the presence of

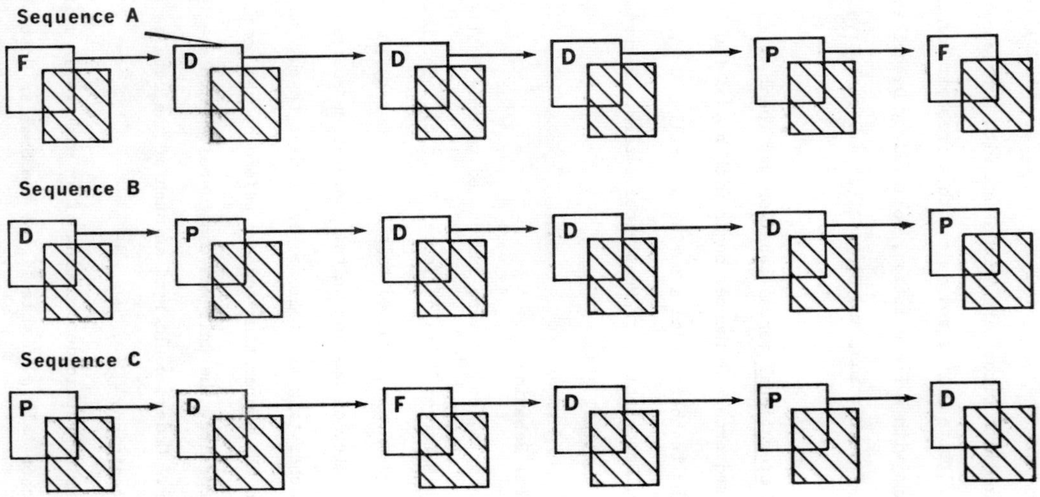

Key

F—Focusing Operation
D—Descriptive Operation
P—Prescriptive Operation
Diagonal lines represent Substantive Areas

Figure 3

Model of Typical Sequences of Operational Verbal Behavior

136

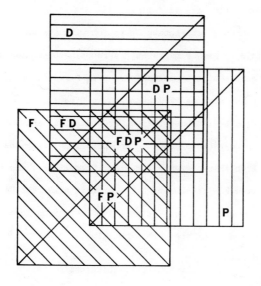

Key

    F--Focusing Operation
    D--Descriptive Operation
    P--Prescriptive Operation

Larger diagonal line separates Operations
   and Substantive Areas

Figure 4

A Tentative Model Describing a Larger Unit of Individualized
Verbal Teaching Behavior of Cooperating Teachers in
Conference with Student Teachers

Operational and Substantive variables. There are three squares. Square
represents a Focusing Operation. Square D represents a Descriptive Oper-
tion and Square P, a Prescriptive Operation. Within the uninterrupted te
presented here there are seven possibilities for the Larger Units of
Verbal Behavior. They are as follows:

Area D shows a Descriptive Operation with its accompanying Substa-
tive Dimension(s). Area F represents a Focusing Operation with its
accompanying Substantive Dimension(s). Area P represents a Prescriptive
Operation with its accompanying Substantive Dimension(s). Area D represents a larger unit with Descriptive, Prescriptive, and Substantive Dimensions. Area FD represents Focusing and Describing with the Substantive
Dimensions. Area FP represents Focusing, Prescribing, and the Substanti-
Dimensions. Area FDP represents a Larger Unit of Verbal Behavior contair-
ing Focusing, Descriptive and Prescriptive Operations accompanied by the
Substantive Dimension of the verbal behavior.

Quantitative Findings

Quantitative presentation of the data includes a description of
(1) the frequency of Operational categories; (2) frequency of Substantive
categories; and (3) a description of the sequence of Operational categori-
Data used in this phase of the study were typescripts of nine conferences
of six cooperating teachers systematically selected from the total eighte-
conferences.

Frequency of Operational Categories

The total number of Operational categories in the nine conferences was 1,068. The range of frequency of Operational talk in the conference was from a low of thirty-three to a high of 301, with a median of 106 and a mean of 119. Table I presents the quantitative findings describing the Operations used by six cooperating teachers in nine conferences. This range of Operational talk suggests that cooperating teachers' conferences were not the same in number of operations used.

Cooperating teachers whose conferences had more Operational units also had the longest conferences, and the teachers having the least number of units had the shortest conferences. Teacher B had the longest conference (fifty-six pages) and teacher E, the shortest (six pages). The average length of a conference was twenty-four pages.

Focusing Operations accounted on the average for 16 percent of the Operational talk. During nine conferences the cooperating teachers' use of this Operation ranged from a high of 21 percent to a low of 8 percent of 169 Focusing Operations.

Descriptive Operations accounted on the average for 67 percent of the Operational talk. The range of use of this category within a total frequency of 739 was from a high of 78 percent by teacher A to a low of 30 percent by teacher E. This finding suggests that cooperating teachers use the Descriptive Operations most frequently.

Prescriptive Operations were found, on the average, to account for 17 percent of the Operational talk. During the conferences the cooperating teachers used 160 Prescriptions, ranging from a high of 49 percent by teacher E to a low of 2 percent by teacher A.

Table I

Number and Percent of Operations Used by Each Cooperating Teacher in a Total of Nine Conferences

Teacher	Code Used to Identify Conference	Focusing N	%	Descriptive N	%	Prescriptive N	%	Total N	%	Number of Pages[a]
A	KC3	15	20.0	59	78.0	2	0.02	76	100.0	24
B	OC2	61	20.0	188	63.0	52	17.00	301	100.0	56
C	SC1	20	16.0	88	70.0	18	14.00	126	100.0	23
C	SC3	18	11.0	131	78.0	18	11.00	167	100.0	32
D	VC1	11	8.0	104	78.0	19	14.00	134	100.0	24
E	WC2	6	14.0	28	65.0	9	21.00	43	100.0	10
E	WC3	7	21.0	10	30.0	16	49.00	33	100.0	6
F	LC2	19	15.0	70	74.0	17	11.00	106	100.0	24
F	LC3	12	18.0	61	66.0	9	16.00	82	100.0	18
Total		169		739		160		1,068		271
Range Number		6-61		10-188		2-52		33-301		6-56
Range Percent		8.0-21.0		30.0-78.0		.02-49.00				
Mean		19	16.0	82	67.0	18	17.02	119		30

[a]Each page consisted of twenty-five six-inch lines of typescript.

The findings indicating the frequency with which the cooperating teachers used the Operations suggest that the teachers are generally similar in the amount of time they used the Focusing, Descriptive, and Prescriptive Operations. This finding, however, should be considered with the findings for each one of the six cooperating teachers. (See Table I.)

Frequency of Substantive Areas

Twenty Substantive Areas were identified in the original analysis of the data. Table II presents these areas in rank order. The most frequently used area was Characteristics of Children, occurring 641 times (30.89 percent). The next most frequent areas were Student Teacher Teaching Behavior, occurring 366 times (17.63 percent), Content, occurring 290 times (13.97 percent), Cooperating Teacher Teaching Behavior, occurring 225 times (10.84 percent), and Generalized Teaching Behavior, occurring 146 times (7.03 percent). Following these areas were Instructional Materials, found 128 times (6.16 percent), The Lesson, found 98 times (4.72 percent), Student Teaching Experiences, found 42 times (2.02 percent), Parents, found 25 times (1.25 percent), and Routines, found 22 times (1.06 percent).

The remaining Substantive Areas were found less often and represent the lower half of the rank order. These areas include The Conference, occurring 19 times (0.96 percent), Administrative/Supervisory Behavior, occurring 13 times (0.62 percent), Curriculum, occurring 11 times (0.53 percent), Other Teaching Behavior, occurring eight times (0.38 percent). Professional Sequence, also occurring eight times (0.38 percent), School

Table II

Rank, Number, and Percent of Substantive Areas Used by Six
Cooperating Teachers in a Total of Nine Conferences

Rank	Substantive Area	Number	Percent o Total
1	Characteristics of Children	641	30.89
2	Student Teacher Teaching Behavior	366	17.63
3	Content	290	13.97
4	Cooperating Teacher Teaching Behavior	225	10.84
5	Generalized Teaching Behavior	146	7.03
6	Instructional Materials	128	6.16
7	The Lesson	98	4.72
8	The Student Teaching Experience	42	2.02
9	Parents	25	1.25
10	Routines	22	1.06
11	The Conference	20	0.96
12	Special Teachers	19	0.91
13	Administrative/Supervisory Behavior	13	0.62
14	Curriculum	11	0.53
15	Other Teaching Behavior	8	0.38
16	Professional Sequence	8	0.38
17	School Monitor	7	0.33
18	Community Agencies	3	0.14
19	A Plan for Teaching	1	0.04
20	School Nurse	1	0.04
	Total	2,075	99.90

Monitor, occurring seven times (0.33 percent), Community Agencies, occurring three times (0.14 percent), A Plan for Teaching, occurring one time (0.04 percent), and School Nurse, occurring one time (0.04 percent).

The range of use is broad, beginning with the single instance of 0.04 percent of the total 2,075 instances of use to an occurrence of 641, or 30.89 percent of use. The first ten most frequently used areas represent substantitive talk which took place in most conferences. The lower half of the ranking includes areas which were used infrequently by only one or two teachers or very few times by a number of teachers. Table III presents the number and percent of use of Substantive Areas for each cooperating teacher.

Individual cooperating teacher's use of the Substantive Areas ranged from a high of 480 for Teacher B in the second conference to a low of seventy-six for Teacher E in the third conference (see Table III). The median number of areas used was 230 and the mean was 230.5. This range suggests that cooperating teachers vary in the frequency of use of the Substantive Areas.

The Sequence of Operations

Operational sequences included sequence combinations of Operational Verbal Behavior used by cooperating teachers in the conferences. The findings presented here describe the frequency with which the operational sequences were found in a systematically selected sample of the Cooperating Teachers' Verbal Behavior. The sample represents fifteen consecutive Larger Units of Verbal Behavior. The presentation includes an explanation of a matrix describing the sequences and a quantitative description of the

Table III

Number and Percent of Substantive Areas Used by
Six Teachers in a Total of Nine Conferences

	Substantive Areas	A		B		C	
				Cooperating Teachers			
1	Characteristics of Children	43	27.04	118	24.58	87	32.5
2	Student Teacher	24	15.09	122	25.41	33	12.3
3	Content	24	15.09	60	12.50	41	15.3
4	Cooperating Teacher Teaching Behavior	28	17.61	37	07.70	37	13.8
5	Generalized Teaching Behavior	12	07.54	33	06.87	21	07.8
6	Instructional Materials	14	08.80	41	08.54	16	05.9
7	The Lesson	8	05.03	25	05.20	10	03.7
8	The Student Teaching Experience	2	01.25	6	01.25	6	02.2
9	Parents	-	-	8	01.66	-	-
10	Routines	2	01.25	7	01.45	-	-
11	The Conference	-	-	3	00.62	3	01.1
12	Special Teachers	-	-	-	-	3	01.1
13	Administrative/Supervisory Behavior	-	-	6	01.25	3	01.1
14	Curriculum	1	00.62	2	00.41	1	00.3
15	Other Teacher Behavior	-	-	2	00.41	5	01.8
16	The Professional Sequence	-	-	3	00.62	1	00.3
17	School Monitor	-	-	6	01.25	-	-
18	Community Agencies	-	-	1	00.20	-	-
19	A Plan for Teaching	-	-	-	-	-	-
20	School Nurse	-	-	-	-	-	-
	Total	159		480		267	

C	D	E	E	F	F	Total All Conferences
124 40.65	77 33.47	37 31.62	20 26.31	43 26.06	92 39.82	641 30.89
41 11.71	20 08.69	14 11.96	23 30.26	43 26.06	46 19.91	366 17.63
60 17.14	8 03.47	22 18.80	9 11.84	35 21.21	31 13.41	290 13.97
33 09.42	31 13.47	20 17.09	6 07.89	7 04.24	26 11.25	225 10.84
11 03.14	46 06.08	9 07.69	2 02.63	2 01.21	10 04.32	146 07.03
25 07.14	2 00.86	7 05.98	8 10.52	8 04.84	7 03.03	128 06.16
14 04.00	14 06.08	4 03.41	1 01.31	11 06.66	11 04.76	98 04.72
7 02.00	10 04.34	- -	1 01.31	9 05.45	1 00.43	42 02.02
17 04.85	- -	- -	- -	- -	1 00.43	25 01.25
2 00.17	2 00.68	3 02.56	4 05.26	2 01.21	- -	22 01.06
4 01.14	- -	- -	- -	3 01.81	3 01.29	20 00.96
1 00.28	15 06.52	- -	- -	- -	- -	19 00.91
1 00.28	3 01.30	- -	- -	- -	- -	13 00.62
4 01.14	2 00.86	- -	- -	- -	1 00.43	11 00.53
1 00.28	- -	- -	- -	- -	- -	8 00.38
2 00.57	- -	- -	- -	- -	- -	8 00.38
- -	- -	- -	- -	1 00.60	- -	7 00.33
2 00.57	- -	- -	- -	- -	- -	3 00.14
1 00.28	- -	- -	- -	- -	- -	1 00.04
- -	- -	- -	- -	1 00.60	- -	1 00.04
350	230	117	76	165	231	2,075 99.90

frequencies of Operational Sequences. Figure 5 presents a matrix which can be used for conceptualizing the frequency of Operational Sequences in a sample of verbal behavior from nine conferences.

There are nine cells within the matrix which represent the pattern of Operational verbal behavior found in the conferences. The first cell (FF) represents two Smaller Units of Verbal Behavior in which a Focusing Operation was followed by another Focusing Operation. The second cell (FD) represents two smaller units in which a Focusing Operation was followed by a Descriptive Operation. The third cell (FP) shows Focusing followed by a Prescriptive Operation. The remaining six cells represent Descriptive followed by Focusing (DF), Descriptive followed by Descriptive (DD), Descriptive followed by Prescriptive (DP), Prescriptive followed by Focusing (PF), Prescriptive followed by Descriptive (PD), and Prescriptive followed by Prescriptive (PP). Each tally in each cell represents two units of verbal behavior found sequentially in the flow of cooperating teacher talk. By recording the flow of talk in this manner it was possible to present a graphic representation of the quantitative nature of the sequential cooperating teacher Operational behavior described by the model in Figure 4.

The matrix indicates that the six cooperating teachers in the nine conferences most frequently described the nature of the Substantive Areas under discussion and followed this type of talk by further Descriptive talk related to the Substantive Areas under discussion. The matrix also indicates that these cooperating teachers least frequently focused upon a Substantive Area and followed their Focus with a Prescriptive Operation. Other cells in the matrix represent other patterns found in the conference

FF	FD	FP
///// //	///// /////	///// /
	///// ////	

DF	DD	DP
///// /////	///// /////	///// /////
///// /////	///// /////	///// //
	///// /////	
	///// /////	
	///// /////	
	///// /////	

PF	PD	PP
///// /////	///// /////	///// /////
///	///// /	//

Figure 5

Matrix for Conceptualizing the Frequency of Operational
Sequences in a Sample of Verbal Behavior from
Nine Cooperating Teachers' Conferences

Table IV presents the quantitative findings related to the pattern of Operational Sequences found in the matrix. The most frequent sequence (DD) occurred in 35 percent of the sample which was analyzed. The least frequent sequence (FP) occurred in 3.5 percent of the sample. Further examination of these findings suggests that most Operational Sequences occur in the ranges nearest the mean and median. This finding suggests that there was a variety of Operational Sequences occurring as cooperating teachers discussed the Substantive Areas.

A Comparison of Two Category Systems

The findings presented here deal with the comparison of the system of categories developed to describe the verbal behavior of cooperating teachers with the categories developed by Brown-Hoffman, which were used to describe the verbal behavior of college supervisors in conferences with student teachers. (See Chapter IV.) Data used for the comparison were fifteen consecutive Larger Units of Verbal Behavior systematically selected from nine college supervisors' conferences with student teachers, and fifteen consecutive Larger Units of Verbal Behavior from nine systematically selected cooperating teacher conferences. The following questions provided the framework for the presentation of the findings:

> When the system of categories describing the verbal behavior of cooperating teachers is applied to the data on the college supervisor, do the categories account for all the verbal behavior?
>
> What behaviors are used most by the cooperating teachers?
>
> What behaviors are used most by the college supervisors?
>
> Which behaviors are similar?

148

Table IV

Frequency of Operational Sequences in a Sample of
Verbal Behavior in Nine Cooperating
Teachers' Conferences

Operational Sequence	Number	Percent of Use
DD	60	35.0
DF	20	12.0
FD	19	11.1
DP	17	10.0
PD	16	9.4
PF	13	8.0
PP	12	7.0
FF	7	4.0
FP	6	3.5

	Total	170		100.0
Range	High	Median	Mean	Low
Number	60	16	19	9
Percent	35.0	9.4	11.1	3.5

Cooperating Teacher Data Analyzed
by the Brown-Hoffman System

Table V presents the quantitative findings related to the analysis
of cooperating teacher data using the Brown-Hoffman System. In analyzing
the cooperating teacher data, using the Brown-Hoffman categories, it was
found that all of the verbal behavior could be classified. Not all of the
categories, however, were used in the analysis. They were: Administrative

Procedures and Leading Procedures, which fall in the Structuring Domain, and Catharsis Procedures and Social Amenities Procedures, which fall in the Affective Domain.

Table V

Number and Percent of Use of Brown-Hoffman Categories from a
Sample of Cooperating Teacher Data

Category	Number	Percent
A2a	53	30.1
A1b	39	22.2
A2b	29	16.5
A1a	22	12.5
B2	19	10.8
C2b	13	07.4
C1b	1	00.5
C1a	-	-
C2a	-	-
B1	-	-
B3	-	-
Total	176	100.0

The other eight categories were identified. These categories appeared in the cooperating teacher data with frequencies ranging from 30.1 percent to 00.5 percent. Interpreting Evaluating Procedures appeared most frequently. The next three most frequent categories were: Defining

Procedures (22.2 percent), Hypothesizing Procedures (16.5 percent), and
Identifying Procedures (12.5 percent). These four categories are
classifications of verbal behavior which Brown-Hoffman have described as
falling in the Problem-Solving Domain. As analyzed by this investigator,
81.3 percent of the cooperating teacher data sample of verbal behavior was
classified within this Domain.

Rapport-Building Procedures accounted for 10.8 percent of the data.
This was the only procedure classified within the Affective Domain.
Controlling Procedures accounted for 7.4 percent of the data and Summary
Procedures accounted for 00.5 percent. These two categories fall within
the Structuring Domain.

College Supervisor Data
Analyzed by the Tentative Model

Table VI presents the quantitative findings related to the analysis
of college supervisors' verbal behavior, using the categories established
by this investigator to describe the verbal behavior of cooperating
teachers. In analyzing the data it was found that not all of the verbal
behavior of the college supervisor could be classified. All of the
Operational Categories were used in the analysis, but not all of the
Substantive Areas which appeared in the cooperating teacher data appeared
in the college supervisor data. It was also found that there were
Substantive Areas occurring in the college supervisor data which did not
appear in the cooperating teacher data.

The two Substantive Areas found in the college supervisors' data
were The Recording (RC) and The College Supervisor (CS).

The Recording. The Recording referred to the procedures used by

Table VI

Number and Percent of Use of Categories of Cooperating Teacher
Verbal Behavior from a Sample of College Supervisor Data

Code for College Supervisor	Operations						Substantive Areas							
	FO	DS	PR	SB	CC	CT	LM	IM	CB	RC	CS	GB	CF	PN
CMC1	4	6	1	3	3	3	0	3	2	1	6	0	0	0
OFC4	6	4	1	7	10	1	0	0	0	0	0	0	0	0
BMC4	6	5	1	10	9	1	0	0	1	0	0	2	0	0
BKC5	1	8	6	14	8	5	4	0	0	0	0	1	0	0
CLC1	2	7	4	12	2	1	3	8	2	1	0	0	0	0
CCC1	4	2	2	6	4	7	1	0	1	1	0	0	1	0
WAC4	5	7	1	7	6	6	1	0	0	0	0	0	0	0
WKC1	4	4	1	5	1	0	4	0	0	4	0	0	1	0
MCC4	7	7	1	8	10	2	1	0	2	0	0	0	0	1
Total	39	50	18	72	53	26	14	11	8	7	6	3	2	1
Percent	36	47	17	36.0	26.1	13.0	07.0	05.0	04.0	03.4	03.0	01.0	01.0	00.5

the college supervisor to tape-record the teaching of the student teachers with whom they were having the conference. This recording was used as part of the conference framework for focusing on the analysis of the teaching which the student had done.

The College Supervisor. The College Supervisor referred to talk appearing in the conference which dealt with reference to the college supervisor. This area was used by one college supervisor as he referred to his analysis of the student's lesson and to his talks with the cooperating teacher working with the student.

Findings from the analysis of the college supervisor conference indicate that college supervisors used the Focusing Operation (FO) in 36.4 percent of the Operational Talk. Descriptive Operations (DS) occurred in 47.0 percent of the total Operations, and the Prescriptive Operations (PR) were found in 17.0 percent of the talk.

These findings suggest that the college supervisor spent more of the conference time in Focusing on the substance of the conference and in using Descriptive Operations related to these Substantive Areas. Prescribing was the least frequent type of Operational Verbal Behavior. Of the three Operations, the Descriptive Category was the most frequently used.

The use of nine Substantive Areas ranged from a high of 36.0 percent for Student Teacher Teaching Behavior (SB) to a low of 00.5 percent for The Plan (PN). The next most frequent areas used by the college supervisors were: Characteristics of Children (CC) (26.1 percent) and Content (CN) (13.0 percent).

Eleven of the Substantive Areas used by cooperating teachers were not used by the college supervisors. Most of the unused areas were areas

153

which fell in the lower rank of use by the cooperating teachers. These were: Special Teachers, Administrative/Supervisory Behavior, Curriculum Other Teacher Behavior, School Monitor, Community Agencies, and School Nurse. Unused areas falling in the upper rank of cooperating teacher use were: The Student Teaching Experience, Parents, and Routines.

A System of Categories for Describing and Analyzing Verbal Teaching Behavior of Cooperating Teachers in Conference with Student Teachers

The model developed in this study is made up of descriptions of verbal teaching behavior of cooperating teachers. Future research should give attention to verification and/or modification of the tentative model developed in this study. A possible modification of the tentative model appears on pages 154-157. The Operations and Substantive Areas have been examined and synthesized into a more detailed and comprehensive model: (1) a more detailed system of code indicators for classifying data; (2) extended descriptions of the Operational categories; (3) synthesis of the Substantive Areas into five major classifications; and (4) sub-classifications of Substantive Areas that provide a possible framework for investigating the specific nature of this dimension of supervisory conferences.

It is important to note that the modification of the categories is not presented as a model of individualized teaching of the same order as the original model. Some of the classifications that appear in the modification constitute categories of individualized supervisory teaching that have not as yet been empirically identified and described in supervisory conferences. The intent here in developing a modification of the tentative model is to formulate an instrument that might possibly be used in the designs of future studies.

The Modified Model: System of Categories for Describing Supervisory Teaching Behavior

Categories used to classify supervisory teaching describe verbal teaching behavior in supervisory conferences. There are two basic dimensions to these categories. The dimensions are referred to as Operational and Substantive.

Operational Verbal Behavior

One dimension of verbal behavior identified in supervisory conferences is Operational. This type of teaching is functional and is classified in three ways. The three functions of Operational behavior are: Focusing, Descriptive, and Prescriptive.

Focusing Operations. Focusing Operations indicate verbal behavior that calls attention to or denotes the Substantive Areas to be discussed in the conference. A Focusing Operation solicits or refers to the substance of the supervisory discourse at different and varying levels of thought. A supervisor Focuses by means of a question or reference to a definition, an explanation, an inference, a logical relationship, a proposal or hypothesis, a generalization, an evaluation, an agreement or disagreement, a re-statement, or a reaction.

Referring means to denote, allude, or initiate.

Asking means to inquire, examine, solicit, invite or investigate.

Code Indicators for Classifying Focusing Operations

Focusing (FO)

FO1.0   Refers

1.1	Refers to a definition or description
1.2	Refers to an explanation
1.3	Refers to an inference
1.4	Refers to a logical relationship
1.5	Refers to a summary
1.6	Refers to a proposal or hypothesis
1.7	Refers to a generalization
1.8	Refers to an evaluation

1.9   Refers to a reaction
1.10 Refers to an agreement or disagreement
1.11 Refers to a re-statement

FO2.0   Asks

2.1   Asks for a definition or description
2.2   Asks for an explanation
2.3   Asks for an inference
2.4   Asks for a logical relationship
2.5   Asks for a summary
2.6   Asks for a proposal or hypothesis
2.7   Asks for a generalization
2.8   Asks for an evaluation
2.9   Asks for a reaction
2.10 Asks for an agreement or disagreement
2.11 Asks for a re-statement

Descriptive Operations. Descriptive Operations order the phenomen
of the substantive talk. These operations function as a process to bring
meanings, clarifications, feelings, judgements and generalizations to the
content under discussion in a supervisory conference.

Example

Defining means to describe or portray or identify.

Clarifying means to interpret, explain, reason, infer or imply.

Summarizing means to abstract previous discourse.

Agreeing means to accept a position or point of view.

Disagreeing means to not accept a position or point of view.

Restating means to repeat what has been previously said.

Reacting means to reply in a subjective way.

Code Indicators for Classifying Descriptive Operations

Descriptive (DS)

DS1.1   Defining

DS1.2   Clarifying

1.21 Explaining
1.22 Making logical relationships
1.23 Inferring or implying

156

DS1.3   Proposing or making a proposition

DS1.4   Hypothesizing

DS1.5   Summarizing

DS1.6   Generalizing (logic not clear)

DS1.7   Generalizing (logic clear)

DS1.8   Agreeing

DS1.9   Disagreeing

DS1.10 Restating

DS1.11 Reacting

Prescriptive Operations. Prescriptive Operations are decisions
made by the supervisor which prescribe the nature of a teaching behavior
that did, will or might have taken place. It may be that subsequent
teaching behaviors that occur as a result of the interaction in a supervisory conference are initiated through the use of these Prescriptive
behaviors. With this in mind, it can be assumed that this Operation may
be considered a crucial teaching behavior for it seems to have an important
influence on the student teacher's subsequent teaching. It also provides
the framework for the quality of productive and generative knowledge
related to concepts of teaching behaviors. These Operations may develop
at a very low level of thought production. Through the use of skillful
and systematic Focusing and Descriptive Operations on the part of the
supervisor higher levels of productive knowledge may be developed. A
Prescriptive Operation classifies only that talk in the conference that
deals with generalizations about teaching behaviors and does not classify
generalizations related to other Substantive Areas.

Examples

To think about or guess the nature of a teaching behavior.

To consider a proposal for a teaching behavior.

To make a proposition for a teaching behavior

To anticipate or hypothesize a teaching behavior.

To generalize a teaching behavior.

Code Indicators for Classifying Prescriptive Operations

Code Indicator

Prescriptive Operations   PR

1.1   Generalizing (no logical referent)   PR

1.2   Considering a proposal (no logical referent)   PR

1.3   Making a proposition (logical referent)   PR

1.4   Hypothesizing (logical ordered plan for testing   PR
             appropriateness of a Prescription--
             There is an inherent assumption that
             this teaching will be examined for
             possible subsequent modification.)

1.5   Generalizing   (logical referent--It is assumed that   PR
             these Prescriptions are concepts of
             teaching and are highly related to
             the prediction about and control of
             teaching.)

Substantive Areas

        The second dimension of verbal behavior in supervisory conferences
is Substantive. A Substantive area identifies what the participants of
the conference are talking about. Each Operational category is accompanie
by at least one Substantive Area.

    Teaching Behaviors   TB

    1.1   Interactive Teaching Behaviors   ITB
          Refers to teaching that takes place in
          individualized, small group, or large
          classroom situations. During this teach-
          ing there occur behavioral processes and
          operations that are verbal, performanative,
          or expressive.

          1.11   Student Teacher   STTB
          1.12   Supervisor   CTTB
          1.13   Generalizations   GTB
          1.14   Other Teachers   OTTB
          1.15   Team Teaching   TTTB

1.2 Schematic Teaching Behaviors   SCB
Deals with teaching behavior such as planning
lessons, units of instruction, establishing
routines, assessment and evaluation of learning. Concerns of the conference participants
falling in this area can be classified as any
teaching behavior that is <u>not</u> interactive.

     1.21 Student Teacher   STTB
     1.22 Supervisor   CTTB
     1.23 Generalizations   GTB
     1.24 Other Teachers   OTTB
     1.25 Team Teaching   TTTB

Background and Characteristics of Learners   CC

Interaction in supervisory conferences focuses on background and characteristics of learners. Both the children
in a classroom and the student teacher himself are discussed. All talk that relates to background and characteristics of any learner falls in this area.

2.1 Cognitive structure   CS
2.2 Social structure   SS
2.3 Psychological structure   PsS
2.4 Physical structure   PyS

Curriculum Content   CN

Deals with the curricula for the elementary school
and the professional education sequence.

3.1 Knowledge   CNK
3.2 Skills   CNS
3.3 Attitudes   CNA

Organization and Administration of Instruction   OA

Concerned with the organization and administration of
instruction in the elementary school and the school of
education preparing the student teacher.

4.1 Instructional   IN
     4.11 Modes   MD
     4.12 Lessons   LN
     4.13 Units   UN
     4.14 Curricula designs   CS

4.2 Administrative   AD
    4.21 Interactive   IT
    4.22 Schematic   SC

Instructional Materials   IM

Focuses on materials of instruction for children and
the student.

5.1 Use of media and materials   UM
5.2 Production of media and materials   PM

Implications and Recommendations

Relationships between independent, intervening, and dependent
variables identified in supervisory conferences should be studied in order
that hypotheses can be tested and confirmed or rejected. These findings
then will eventually provide explanatory principles that can be used to
control and predict the effect of cooperating teachers' individualized
teaching.

For example, investigators should focus their study on the relationships that exist between the cooperating teacher's verbal behavior in conference and the level of thinking evidenced by the student teachers' verbal
behavior. Different modes of supervisory conferences with student teacher
should be studied to gain further knowledge. Answers to the following
questions would lead to the establishment of this knowledge.

> What are the relationships among the use of the categories
> of verbal behavior in different conference situations, such
> as a short conference, a long conference, a student-centered
> conference, a conference focused on the analysis of teaching,
> general conferences, three-way conferences with other individuals
> who have a responsibility to the student teacher's experience,
> and conferences focused on one Substantive Area?

> What variables affect the intent of the cooperating teacher

in structuring the conference? How do these variables affect the verbal behavior in conferences which are structured around a specific intent such as the analysis of the levels of children's thinking on the development of specific concepts?

The findings of this study indicate that cooperating teachers' use of the categories of verbal behavior varied. Future investigators should attempt to understand the dynamics of cooperating teachers' personal teaching styles, strategies, and maneuvers. Investigations of this nature would be fruitful in adding knowledge related to the following questions currently raised by individuals working in the general field of supervision, both pre-service and inservice.

Is there an emerging substance of supervision? Are supervisors using patterns of verbal behavior that might suggest a logic of supervisory discourse? Does the language of supervision reveal characteristic linguistic forms?

Outcomes and effects of the cooperating teachers' work with student teachers are important considerations in understanding the work of the cooperating teacher. Investigations should be developed which attempt to relate verbal teaching behavior to the following outcomes:

Does the cooperating teacher help the student solve his problems? Does the cooperating teacher adapt himself to the students' needs? Has the cooperating teacher developed his own personal idiom? Does the cooperating teacher have a commitment to his own and his student teacher's individual personal idiom?

What are the relationships between a cooperating teacher's verbal teaching behavior in conferences with a student and the student teacher's self acceptance, motivational changes, development of critical thinking, creativity, problem-solving ability, conceptualization of subject matter as instructional fields, and conceptualization of the learning process and methodology?

The comparative phase of this study was fruitful in pointing to

implications for further study of the specific similarities and differen
of the Brown-Hoffman Model and the tentative model developed in this stu

A common data source should be used to analyze more fully the
relationships between the two category systems. Further study of the tw
models should reveal reasons for the lack of appearance of some of the
Brown-Hoffman categories in the cooperating teaching data. Indications
to the reasons for the high percentages of the Brown-Hoffman Problem-
Solving Domain in cooperating teacher data should also be forthcoming
through further investigation.

Further study should be made in an attempt to describe the common
alities and significant differences between the categories of verbal
behavior developed in other studies of teaching in the total classroom
situation with large groups of learners and one teacher and the categori
described in this study. It is important also that team-teaching situat
be systematically studied in order to identify teaching variables. Thes
findings should be compared with group and individualized teaching.

This study was carried out using a limited population of cooperat
teachers, selected classificatory principles in content analysis, one
method of establishing levels of reliability, and a stipulated definitio
of model development. The following implications are suggested as future
extensions of the present design and methodology.

Attempts should be made to investigate and test the feasibility o
the model developed in the present study by designing studies which atte
to deal with variables such as:

        larger populations of cooperating teachers
        different geographic locations
        different philosophical orientations of cooperating teachers

various modes and types of administration and supervision
    of elementary school
types of student teachers
types of college supervisors
age of children or youth being taught
subject matter specialization
judged competencies of cooperating teachers

Classificatory principles in content analysis used in this and other studies of teaching should be investigated in order to establish implications for use and development of these principles in systematic analysis of teaching.

A priori and a posteriori types of content analysis should be compared empirically by analyzing data using categories of verbal teaching behavior developed by the two approaches. Findings may give clues as to the limitations and strengths of the two methods of establishing variables in the first stages of theory development.

Reliability procedures used in the studies of teaching should be examined. It may be possible to postulate criteria for these procedures which can then be tested. Categories of verbal behavior of cooperating teachers should be subjected to analysis by (1) a team of coders with general backgrounds, and (2) by coders with specializations in the substantive areas.

It is assumed that the performance of individuals whose teaching responsibility is in the professional laboratory experience for student teachers has some uniqueness. As has been shown, linguistic variables of supervisory teaching in conferences with students can be identified and analyzed. Programs preparing cooperating teachers should help them to identify and understand the linguistic variables in their individualized teaching, and the relationships of these variables to desired outcomes in

163

the various aspects of their work with a student teacher.

As future investigators verify the existence of the verbal behavior identified in the present study, individuals designing programs to prepare cooperating teachers should endeavor to help teachers to understand the specific functions and patterns of the three Operations described here. Experiences should be provided in which the Focusing Operation is studied in a variety of teaching situations. Similar study of the Descriptive and Prescriptive Operations would be fruitful.

Each of the substantive areas can be studied further by cooperating teachers to determine the form and structure of these areas as they are dealt with during supervisory teaching. As cooperating teachers carry out study of substantive areas, they should begin to formulate a conceptual scheme which would help them in organizing the content of the substantive areas in an appropriate form for the student teacher himself to use in formulating his conceptual scheme of the areas in his future work with children and/or youth.

Cooperating teachers can be taught to use the study of teaching as the central focus in guiding student teachers' laboratory experiences. In order to accomplish this, programs preparing cooperating teachers must resolve the question of the substance of the study of teaching. Inherent in the answer to this question, is the need for a search for various model of process and substance. For example, in studying teaching cooperating teachers might use the inductive methodology of this study. Using such a model cooperating teachers would have the opportunity to identify their personal style of teaching through the identification of specific variable such as the functions and substance inherent in their teaching situation.

In learning to study the teaching of their students, cooperating teachers can discover a conceptual scheme for analyzing the style of their students. Helping the student to understand how he is functioning in his teaching situation holds promise for continuing development of the future teacher.

Selection and evaluation of cooperating teachers can be carried out by school systems and departments of education, in some part, by using the knowledge of the cooperating teacher's abilities, competencies, and interests in developing himself as a supervisor of student teachers, having the control and understanding of his and others' verbal teaching behavior.

Cooperating teachers working with college supervisors need to determine the unique aspects of their work with student teachers. Conferences between cooperating teachers and college supervisors should deal with substantive areas in such a way as to increase the cooperating teacher's understanding and control over the areas he will deal with in his work with the student. This holds true in reverse for the college supervisor. He will modify his teaching in the substantive areas as he gains understanding and control over his unique contribution to the student teacher's growth.

College supervisors should study their conferences with student teachers to gain greater control and understanding of their function in the student teaching experience. Other supervisory personnel who have direct conference contact with student teachers will also find this type of study a fruitful area for improving professional competencies.

Professors of education who plan professional education sequences

would find the examination of the substantive areas of this study a rich
source of content for their programs in preparing teachers. While many of
the areas have traditionally appeared in curricula models for the future
teacher, a modification of structure and organization of the content areas
seems appropriate in terms of the nature of the concerns students discuss
with cooperating teachers.

This final implication provides a framework for possible rethinking
of the content for professional education sequences in teacher education
programs. The focus for the structure of content and experiences aimed at
preparing teachers should be centered around a systematic study of teaching
behaviors. In this way the student of teaching would develop a concept of
himself as a teacher rather than, as heretofore, solely from concepts of
related disciplines. The formulation of a concept of teaching can no
longer be left to chance as has been asked of students of teaching in the
past. In the future prospective teachers should be systematically guided
to formulations of their own personal teaching styles through well planned
and conceived encounters with concepts of teaching.

Chapter VI

THE WORK OF ONE COLLEGE SUPERVISOR WITH COOPERATING TEACHERS

IN OFF-CAMPUS SCHOOLS: AN ANALYSIS OF CONFERENCES

Theodora Randall Kimsey

Change in the locale of student teaching experiences and the many
difficulties which have arisen as a result have caused teacher educators
to become greatly concerned over the relationship between schools and
colleges engaged in teacher education and the quality of the student
teaching experiences being provided. Efforts aimed toward improving
school-college relationships and the quality of student teaching experiences have been stepped up and become more widespread. Many of those
involved have come to believe that the quality of student teaching
experience is conditioned by the guidance given to students during the
student teaching period and this, in turn, is affected by the way in which
supervisors of student teachers work together as they carry out their
responsibilities with student teachers.

It is frequently stated in the literature that supervision of a
student teacher is the "joint" or "shared" responsibility of a cooperating
teacher and a college supervisor. But little attention has been given to
the ways and means of their working together. That is, how and on what
the two supervisors work cooperatively with one another, how the two

coordinate their separate efforts with the student teacher. The way in which college supervisors and cooperating teachers far too often work together in off-campus student teaching situations is described by the AACTE Subcommittee on School-College Relationships in Teacher Education:

> College supervision of student teaching has been a link between the school and the college since the beginning of off-campus student teaching, but it has been a very weak link at best. The college supervisor and the student teacher are usually guests in the classroom. Everyone, including the cooperating teacher, treads easily so as not to upset anybody or anything. The student often feels torn between the positions of the cooperating teacher and those of the college supervisor. The college supervisor has little influence over the classroom program, and the practicing classroom teachers have almost no influence over the college program. Both groups tend to go their own ways and no bridges are crossed, no barrier broken, although everyone is usually polite, at least when the other one is around.[1]

Ward and Suttle state: "It is not uncommon for one supervisor to observe and decide upon an approach to helping the student while the other supervisor is pursuing a different one. Both may have equally good approaches they may be simply taking different routes toward the same goal. But when this occurs, it may result in confusion to the one being helped; the student wonders whose suggestions he should follow."[2]

Without question greater cooperation and coordination in the supervision of student teachers is needed for instructional improvement. A

---

[1]E. Brooks Smith (chairman), Cooperative Structures in School-College Relationships for Teacher Education: Report Number Two, American Association of Colleges for Teacher Education Subcommittee on School-College Relationships in Teacher Education (Washington, D.C.: American Association of Colleges for Teacher Education, 1965), p. 102.

[2]William Ward and John Suttle, "The Oregon Plan to Improve the Induction Process: The Program to Prepare Supervision Teachers and the Organization of Schools and Colleges to Accommodate the Process," Journal of Teacher Education, 17:448, Winter, 1966.

cooperating teacher and college supervisor share joint responsibility
for supervising a student teacher, that is, for observing, evaluating,
and guiding the development of a student's teaching behavior. Because the
two supervisors are partners in student teacher supervision, innovative
approaches to partnership hold promise for improvement of the quality of
student teaching experiences.

Innovation in supervisory practices should be based on some conceptualization of supervising behavior. The series of studies on supervision of student teachers reported in this monograph is based on the
assumption that supervising behavior and teaching behavior are, in essence,
the same. Cooperating teachers and college supervisors do individualized
teaching during their supervisory conferences with student teachers. If
one accepts this assumption, that the behavior of the two supervisors with
student teachers during supervisory conferences is teaching behavior, then
the partner relationship between the cooperating teacher and the college
supervisor is, theoretically if not in actual practice, similar to a team
teaching relationship.

Shaplin defines team teaching as ". . . a type of instructional
organization, involving teaching personnel and the students assigned to
them, in which two or more teachers are given responsibility, working
together, for all or a significant part of the instruction of the same
group of students."[1] Explaining more fully the meaning of certain words
and phrases used in this definition, Shaplin states that his use of type

---

[1]Judson T. Shaplin, "Description and Definition of Team Teaching,"
Team Teaching, Judson T. Shaplin and Henry F. Olds, Jr., editors (New York:
Harper and Row, Publishers, 1964), p. 15.

of instructional organization coupled with given responsibility is meant

to convey the idea that a team teaching organization "has formal status,"

that is, "that it has had delegated to it certain responsibilities, and

that it exercises through its personnel legitimate authority in carrying

out these responsibilities."[1] That teachers are given responsibility . .

for . . . the instruction of the same group of students provides further

support for the idea that responsibility has been delegated formally and

clarifies the relationship between the teachers and the students they

teach.[2] Responsibility means, he says, "the team of teachers has both a

firm measure of autonomy and a duty to provide, through joint effort, an

optimum instructional program for its students."[3] His explanation with

regard to working together is enlightening. He says:

> . . . working together specifies a close working relationship
> among the teachers of a team for planning, instruction, and
> evaluation. Teachers should have common instructional aims
> for the same students and should share the instructional tasks
> which are necessary to carry out these aims. The critical test
> of this relationship is the jointness which is displayed in
> actual classroom instruction. Joint planning may occur at
> the committee or departmental level, but if the teacher
> teaches his students and conducts his own evaluation, the
> conditions of joint instruction are not met.[4]

The literature on student teaching provides evidence, in abundance

that cooperating teachers and college supervisors have been jointly

charged with responsibility for student teacher supervision. Moreover,

colleges and schools engaged in teacher education have delegated to these

supervisors the authority or "measure of autonomy" necessary to carry out

this charge. There is, however, ample evidence that the two supervisors

---

[1]Ibid., p. 16.   [2]Ibid.

[3]Ibid., p. 17.   [4]Ibid.

170

often discharge their responsibilities for student teacher supervision without "working together" as a team; "joint effort" is too infrequently the means utilized in performance of supervisory duties. Even though induction of student teachers into the teaching profession is the goal of both supervisors, specific "instructional aims" are often left unstated; consequently, "instructional tasks" in these regards are seldom shared. Both supervisors usually take responsibility for "actual instruction" of student teachers, but joint planning and/or evaluation sessions preceding or following instruction are less common. The prerequisites for a team teaching relationship are present but implementation of a supervising team is often lacking.

The supervising team in teacher education is, in its form and possible mode of operation, quite similar to what Shaplin describes as the "diagnostic" or "clinical" teams in the field of medicine. According to him, these teams are composed of "specialists from several different fields of medicine, who pool their knowledge and opinions to diagnose the ailments of the patient and to propose a strategy of treatment."[1] Responsibility for treatment is delegated to and carried out separately by various members of the team according to area of specialization, but "coordination and planning is achieved," he says, "through case conferences which are held by the team."[2] The purpose and objectives of case conferences held by the clinical team in medicine appear to be markedly

---

[1]Judson T. Shaplin, "Toward a Theoretical Rationale for Team Teaching," Team Teaching, Judson T. Shaplin and Henry F. Olds, Jr., editors (New York: Harper and Row, Publishers, 1964), p. 62.

[2]Ibid.

similar to the possible purpose and objectives of supervisory conferences
held by the supervising team in teacher education.

The objectives of these supervisory conferences between the cooper-
ing teacher and the college supervisor, as identified by the investigator
are:

1. determining the student teacher's present status with
   respect to learning how to teach,

2. planning for the student teacher's future progress with
   regard to becoming a teacher,

3. keeping one another informed of the supervisory actions
   each had taken with the student teacher,

4. planning the supervisory actions each will take with the
   student teacher, and

5. sharing professional information pertinent to supervision
   of student teachers.

Purpose

The study being reported here examined the verbal behavior of the
college supervisor and cooperating teacher as they worked together during
supervisory conferences. The purpose of the study was to develop a model
a system of categories, which could be used to identify and classify the
types of actions taken, the kinds of operations performed, and the variou
topics discussed by the college supervisor and cooperating teacher during
the supervisory conferences which they have with one another. Further,
the system was to be used in describing, quantitatively, the verbal behav
of the supervisors who participated in the study; and quantitative findin
were to be interpreted in relation to functions served or objectives of
the supervisory conferences which provided data for the study.

Design and Methodology

The subjects of the study were one college supervisor and six cooperating teachers serving as supervisors of student teachers enrolled in the Preservice Program at Teachers College, Columbia University. Data for the study were thirty conference tapes, tape recordings of five conferences of the college supervisor with each of the six cooperating teachers.[1]

Three phases of data treatment were used. Phase One, development of the system of analysis using the a posteriori technique for establishing categories, was a two-step process. An audio survey of thirty conference tapes resulted in the identification of indicators of actions, operations, and topics. Analysis in depth of typescripts for six conference tapes[2] resulted in: (1) selection of a unit of analysis for structuring the data; (2) identification of additional indicators of actions, operations, and topics; (3) establishment of three sets of categories which were exhaustive of the data; and (4) formulation of categories within each set which were well adapted to the purposes of the study and mutually exclusive. The two steps in this phase of data analysis produced a system of analysis composed of sets of categories in three

---

[1] The college supervisor tape recorded these conferences with cooperating teachers over a period of ten weeks. The conferences were held during the college supervisor's regular, biweekly visit to the school; conferences immediately followed observation of a lesson taught by the student teacher assigned to the cooperating teacher and preceded the college supervisor's conference with the student.

[2] One conference tape was selected systematically from each set of five conference tapes with each of the six cooperating teachers and verbatim typescripts of this stratified sample were prepared.

dimensions: Interactive Dimension, Logical Dimension, and Substantive Dimension.

Phase Two was establishing the reliability of the categories with each dimension of the system. Data used in testing the reliability of categories were verbatim typescripts for six conference tapes.[1] Ten one-page samples were selected at random from each of the six protocols. The lines or talk on each sample page were coded, and 160 items were selected systematically to test the reliability of categories. Three impartial judges participated in testing the reliability of the category system. The average percent of agreement of all judges with the investigator for the categories in each dimension ranged from .85 to .96. These results compared favorably with Berelson's findings with regard to the reliability of systems of analysis.[2]

In Phase Three of data treatment, application of the system of analysis to selected data, typescripts for six sets of conferences[3] were used. Typescripts were coded by the investigator, using the categories which had been formulated and tested for reliability. Statistical analysis of typescript codings was accomplished through the use of an electronic computer. The results of this analysis were used in the subsequent

---

[1] One conference tape was systematically selected from each set of the four remaining conference tapes with each of the six cooperating teachers.

[2] Bernard Berelson, Content Analysis in Communication Research (Glencoe, Illinois: University of Chicago, The Free Press, 1952), p. 172

[3] Each set included two conferences between the college supervisor one cooperating teacher. (These typescripts of conference tapes were the six which had been used in development of the system of analysis and the six used in establishment of the reliability of the category system.)

quantification of data.

System of Analysis

The major finding of the study was the model, the system of categories which was developed for describing and analyzing the verbal behavior of the cooperating teacher and college supervisor as they worked together during supervisory conferences. The unit of analysis, the three dimensions of the system, and the categories or general topics for categories in each dimension are defined and illustrated in the following.

Unit of Analysis

The unit of analysis for structuring the data in this study was a Speaker Communication Unit. A communication unit by a speaker may consist of one or more words, phrases, and/or sentences which can be classified according to a category within each of the three dimensions of the system of analysis. A speaker communication unit continues as long as there is no change in classification of category within any one of the three dimensions. The uninterrupted talk of a speaker may contain several communication units. Utterances which cannot be classified as to a category in each of the three dimensions are considered noncommunicating and are, therefore, treated as noncodable.

Examples of the uninterrupted talk of the college supervisor (CS) and a cooperating teacher (CT) subdivided (//) into speaker communication units appear below:

> CS   It seemed to me that he [student teacher] was asking some
>   fairly good questions.//Many of the children were eager
>   to respond.//Then he asked this question, "What would
>   you have done if you had been someone back in history

and this had happened?"//One boy wanted to know when this had happened.//He told him, "It happened in 1733."//Then he wrote the date on the blackboard.//

CT She [student teacher] is particularly fond of two children in the class.//I'm going to talk to her about this today.// I think she shouldn't make allowances for these two.// They're always doing something; they're active children, constantly moving, fiddling with their papers.//

Dimensions of the System

The system of analysis is composed of categories within three dimensions: Interactive Dimension, Logical Dimension, and Substantive Dimension.

Interactive Dimension. During the supervisory conference the talk of one speaker has an effect on the talk of the other speaker, that is, an action by one speaker may produce a reciprocal action on the part of the other speaker. Actions and reciprocal actions by the speakers cause the talk to move alternately back and forth between the two speaker The four categories which may be used in coding a communication unit in the Interactive Dimension are: Stating, Completing, Questioning, and Reacting.

Logical Dimension. During the supervisory conference the two speakers say different things about the topics which they discuss, that is, a variety of logical operations can be performed by speakers in con- nection with a subject matter. The four categories which may be used in coding a communication unit in the Logical Dimension are: Reports, Evaluations, Prescriptions, and Plans.

Substantive Dimension. During supervisory conferences the two speakers discuss various topics, i.e., speaker communication units are about something, have a subject matter. Six general topics are used to organize the 33 categories which may be used in coding a communication unit in the Substantive Dimension. General topics for categories are: Supervising Behavior, Teaching Behavior, Student Teachers, Children, Curriculum/Materials, and Situational Information. A model of the system of analysis is presented in Figure 1.

Interactive Dimension Categories

In the following, definitions of the four categories in the Interactive Dimension are presented. Behavioral illustrations, drawn from protocols, are provided for each category.

Stating (STA).[1] Stating actions serve the function of _giving information_ about something. Stating actions may initiate talk about something, may continue the talk about something, and/or may be in response to a question seeking information about something.

Examples:

At first I simply started writing down what she was doing, and the first thing I wanted to say//when she was developing this idea of many different ways of showing this irregularity, most of it was happening just by discussion.//I think that it would have been helpful, clearer to the children about these differ- ent ideas of irregularity which she brought out, if she had made a chart on the board and put some of those words that they discussed on it.//	CS/STA CS/STA CS/STA
What do you mean when you say she's conscientious?//	CS/QUS
Well, she comes early in the mornings, has come before I get here.//She's reading the books that the children are reading so she will be familiar	CT/STA

---

[1]Letters appearing in parentheses after each category label are the symbols which were used in coding data for quantification.

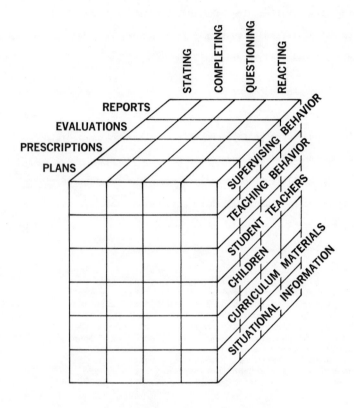

Figure 1

Model for Analyzing and Describing the Verbal Behavior of the
Cooperating Teacher and College Supervisor During
Supervisory Conferences

with them when they meet with her individually.//   CT/STA

Completing (COM). Completing actions serve the function of completing, summarizing and/or adding to an informational statement about
something. Completing actions continue the talk about something, e.g., a
Stating action begun by one speaker may be completed by the other speaker,
and/or a Stating action begun by one speaker may be completed by the same
speaker after being interrupted by a Stating or Completing action by
either speaker.

Examples:

I think he should develop that through//   CT/STA

Sixteenths, at least.//   CS/COM

She was the best student teacher I've ever had;//   CT/STA
and I've had, let's be very conservative, at least
twenty student teachers;//but she was the best,   CT/STA
the most outstanding.//   CT/COM

I write down what I'm going to stress in one
particular lesson, what the lesson might be for
the day, or//   CT/STA

The content rather than//   CS/COM

Or the aims, what might be the overall aims for the
week rather than for each particular lesson.//   CT/COM

Statements which give information often include material concerned
with the relationship of one thing to something else, i.e., the reason for,
purpose of, and/or effects of something. Statements which have the form
of "If . . . then," "This . . . because," and "This . . . so that" may be
completed after being interrupted by a Stating or Completing action.

Examples:

She could have read a list of words and put down
the initial consonant letters//   CT/STA

So that the children could have heard these sounds
and thought about these sounds.//   CS/CO

If he has never been used to going to school//   CS/ST

He's undisciplined.//   CT/ST

Then he probably finds the restrictions that you have
to have in class unbelievable.//   CS/CO

Questioning (QUS). Questioning actions serve the function of
seeking information about something. Questioning actions may initiate
talk about something, continue the talk about something, and/or interrupt
the talk about something by calling for additional information in order
that the talk may continue with greater clarity. A Questioning action is
often used to confirm a hypothesis, inference, or conjecture about
something.

Examples:

When did you say you were going to the police academy?//   CS/QUS

November 28.//   CT/ST

And that will be connected with modern New York?//   CS/QUS

Your group though, this group is a much more calm
group than the group last year, right?//   CS/QUS

Yes, they really are.//   CT/STA

Different ability level?//   CS/QUS

Their reading ability is a little higher, probably
in other areas, math, maybe not; but their reading
is about a year higher.//   CT/STA

Reacting (REA). Reacting actions serve the function of showing
agreement with or approval of the information given about something.
Reacting actions may follow a Stating action or a Completing action, but

they may not follow a Questioning action. Reacting actions are always
unsolicited.

Examples:

Was this a play that some of the other children had done?//	CS/QUS
No, professionally done.//	CT/STA
Oh, wonderful.//	CS/REA

We have a tendency to stop developing these skills too soon because we think that if the children can read and more or less comprehend on a factual level that the need for reading skills is over.//	CS/STA
I know.//	CT/REA

She smiled a great deal.//	CS/STA
Yes.//	CT/REA
She obviously enjoys working with them.//	CS/STA
Yes, she does.//	CT/REA

Reacting actions may occur during the flow of a Stating action.
Since the Reacting actions do not interrupt the flow of the Stating action,
i.e., seem only to encourage the speaker to continue giving information
about something, the Reacting actions are not interpreted as being inter-
ruptive of the action in process. Reacting actions of this type are coded
as a single Reacting action after the action in process has been completed.

Examples:

Also, you know, when they were working on one
of those new ones, if she had asked the children,
"Can you think of any other words that begin with
this same blend?"

Yes.//

then she would have brought more children in and
they would have heard this sound more and more,
and little things like that for extending activity.//   CS/STA
                                                          CT/REA

If as they were introduced, she had simply taped
them on the blackboard, then this would have caught
the children's eyes

Yes.

and kept the words before them.//   CS/STA

Yes.//   CT/REA

Logical Dimension Categories

The following presents definition of the four categories in the

Logical Dimension and behavioral illustrations, drawn from protocols, for

each category.

Reports (REPT). Reports are concerned with factual and analytical

information about the world, what is in the present or what was in the

past and/or what one thinks or has thought with regard to what is or was

in the world.

To report is to describe, generalize, and/or interpret (give an

inference, conjecture, hypothesis, and/or explanation with regard to) an

event, action, person, or state of affairs in the present or in the past.

Examples:

Now this is the book you're using for the
skills development, right?//   CS/QUS/REPT

Yes, it is.//You see we have an individualized   CT/STA/REPT
reading program.//I usually choose one reader   CT/STA/REPT
a little above the level of many of them so that
they can have a little exercise, and I use that
with everybody to develop skills.//   CT/STA/REPT

Comprehension skills and//   CS/COM/REPT

Comprehension and others, interpretation and
finding details.// CT/COM/REPT

Yes.// CS/REA/REPT

Evaluations (EVAL). Evaluations are concerned with a speaker's
judgment with regard to the quality, value, or worth of something in the
world, past or present. Evaluations may or may not include the reasons
for holding a judgment regarding the quality, value, or worth of something.

To evaluate is to rate or grade (use value words of comparative
form of sentence structure to describe) an event, action, person, or state
of affairs in the present or in the past.

Examples:

She has developed, it seems to me, quite a good
understanding of subject matter content, especially
in the science area and in math and reading.// CS/STA/EVAL

I was thinking back to the last time I was here
watching her teach.//Today she was much more at CS/STA/REPT
ease and she displayed more of a sense of humor.// CS/STA/EVAL

Prescriptions (PRES). Prescriptions are concerned with a speaker's
opinion with regard to what could or should have been in the present or in
the past. Prescriptions may or may not include reasons for, purpose of,
or effects which would have been achieved by that which is prescribed.

To prescribe is to suggest what could or should have been with
regard to an event, action, person, or state of affairs in the present or
in the past.

Examples:

She could have said, "Will someone bring their
ruler and come up here and hold it against this
yardstick. Now do we still have enough room for
another child to come up and bring their ruler?"// CS/STA/PRES

Since she was trying to bring out the idea of
different irregular forms such as doubling the
consonants and changing the "y" to "i"//   CS/STA/PRE

She should have had the completely irregular
ones along with it.//   CT/COM/PRE

Why didn't she have <u>more</u> and <u>most</u>?//   CS/QUS/PRE

She should have had all types in the assignment.//   CT/STA/PRE

<u>Plans</u> (PLAN). Plans are concerned with <u>a speaker's opinion with</u>
<u>regard to what can, might, or will be in the future</u>. Plans may or may no
include reasons for, purposes of, or effects which might or will be
achieved by that which is planned.

To plan is to suggest what can, might, or will be with regard to a
event, action, person, or state of affairs in the future.

Examples:

Why don't I start coming on Fridays
at eleven?//   CS/QUS/PLA

Eleven will be fine.//   CT/STA/PLA

I'll be back then on the twenty-sixth at eleven,
then every other week.//   CS/STA/PLA

So, she's really ready to start in on//   CS/STA/PLA

Gathering material//   CT/COM/PLA

And lesson planning and teaching procedures.//   CS/COM/PLA

Substantive Dimension General
Topics for Categories

The following presents definition of the six general topics used
to organize the thirty-three categories in the Substantive Dimension and
provides behavioral illustrations for some of the categories falling under

each general topic.[1]

Supervising Behavior. The general topic, Supervising Behavior, was used to organize any information about the work or behavior of cooperating teachers and college supervisors with student teachers and/or with other supervisors of student teachers. Categories falling under this heading include general and specific information about the role and responsibilities of supervisors, such as: (1) the nature of supervising behavior; (2) reasons for, purposes of, effects of supervisory behavior; and (3) feelings or concerns of supervisors about their work with student teachers. Categories also include general and specific information about what supervisors do, did, or will do with student teachers and/or other supervisors of student teachers. General and specific information about supervising behavior is classified by use of twelve categories.[2]

---

[1]For definition and behavioral illustration of each category in the Substantive Dimension, see Theodora Randall Kimsey, "The Work of One College Supervisor with Cooperating Teachers in Off-Campus Schools: An Analysis of Conferences" (unpublished Ed.D. dissertation, Teachers College, Columbia University, New York, 1969), pp. 56-71.

[2]These twelve categories and the symbols used in coding data are:
Cooperating Teacher Supervising Behavior:
    General ($CTSB_G$)
    Student ($CTSB_{ST}$)
    Students ($CTSB_{STS}$)
    Concerns ($CTSB_C$)
    Observation/Conference ($CTSB_{O/C}$)
College Supervisor Supervising Behavior:
    General ($CSSB_G$)
    Student ($CSSB_{ST}$)
    Students ($CSSB_{STS}$)
    Concerns ($CSSB_C$)
    Observation/Conference ($CSSB_{O/C}$)
Cooperating Teacher/College Supervisor
    Supervising Behavior Team (CT-CSSBT)
Supervising Behavior General (SBG)

Examples:

When she came in today I read her plans, and I
went over her plans with her; and where I could
suggest, I did.//   CT/STA/REPT/CTSB$_G$

When she asked me this morning about what
kinds of questions to use for evaluation,
I told her, "Well, first you will want to
find out from the children what information
they got from the committee report." And I
told her that would serve more than one purpose; it would show, first, whether the children had got enough information, and secondly,
how well they were listening.//   CT/STA/REPT/CTSB$_{ST}$

I told the students that this [making picture
story books] would be good for children who
were less able and had difficulty with writing, at least they could show what ideas they
had obtained.//   CS/STA/REPT/CSSB$_{STS}$

I wrote over here in my notes, "Children
paying close attention during this activity;
activity requires quick behavioral responses,
and all want to be chosen; teacher did not
need to remind children to pay attention."
The reason I wrote all of that was because
I wanted her to think about the kind of
activity that got their attention and held
it.//   CT/STA/REPT/CSSB$_{O/C}$

Teaching Behavior. The general topic, Teaching Behavior, was used

to organize any information about the work or behavior of teachers and

student teachers in the elementary school. Categories falling under this

heading include general and specific information about the teacher role,

such as: (1) the nature of teaching behavior; (2) reasons for, purposes

of, effects of teaching behavior; and (3) feelings and concerns of teacher

about their work with children. Categories included general and specific

information about the duties and responsibilities of teachers and student teachers, e.g., noon and yard duty, correcting papers, conducting teacher-parent conferences, producing assembly programs, taking children on trips. They also include information about what is, was, or will be taught and/or how something is, was, or will be taught. In addition, categories include any information about the behavior of teachers and student teachers related to the plans and preparations they make in regard to teaching children. General and specific information about teaching behavior is classified by use of nine categories.[1]

Examples:

Since she was trying to bring out the idea of different irregular forms such as doubling the consonants and changing the "y" to "i"//	CS/STA/PRES/STTB$_W$
She should have had the completely irregular ones along with them.//	CT/COM/PRES/STTB$_W$
When she was developing this idea of many different ways of showing this irregularity, most of it was happening just by discussion.//	CS/STA/REPT/STTB$_H$
I think that it would have been helpful, clearer to the children about these different ideas of irregularity which she brought out, if she had made a chart on the board and put some of the words that they discussed on it.//	CB/STA/PRES/STTB$_H$

---

[1]These nine categories and coding symbols are:
Student Teacher Teaching Behavior:
      General (STTB$_G$)
      Planning (STTB$_P$)
      What/Content (STTB$_W$)
      How/Methods (STTB$_H$)
      Language (STTB$_L$)
      Characteristics of Behavior (STTB$_{CH}$)
Cooperating Teacher Teaching Behavior (CTTB)
College Supervisor Teaching Behavior (CSTB)
Teaching Behavior General (TBG)

There was a marvelous warmth in her acceptance of their responses that hadn't been there
before, especially their suggestions about the
wagon. I thought it was really marvelous the
way she laughed and smiled during that; the
stiffness was gone.//   CS/STA/EVAL/STTB$_{CH}$

This is actually the way a good teacher
works; she thinks about the possibilities
but as she works on the unit, she keeps
changing and modifying her plans as new
things come up.//   CS/STA/REPT/TBG

Student Teachers. The general topic, Student Teachers, was used t

organize any information about students who are engaged in student teachi

laboratory experiences. Categories falling under this heading include

general and specific information about student teachers as learners and

the particular problems or difficulties which they have in connection wit

taking the role of the teacher. Categories also include information abou

the personality traits and feelings, educational and experiential back-

ground, future plans, and/or concerns of student teachers. General and

specific information about student teachers is classified by use of six

categories.[1]

Examples:

Some of the students have been having
difficulty in the math area because it
is essential that they be very careful
with the language when they're working
on multiplication and division.//   CS/STA/REPT/STSG

---

[1]The six categories and coding symbols are:
Student Teacher:
    General (ST_G)
    Personal (ST_P)
    Background/Future ($ST_{B/F}$)
    Concerns (ST_C)
    Learner (ST_L)
Student Teachers General (STSG)

This thing about her personality, her lack
of outward animation, is very difficult for
her to do anything about. She's enthusias-
tic inside but it just doesn't show.//   CS/STA/REPT/ST$_P$

I know she wants to be a reading specialist
and has completed most of the requirements
for that.//   CS/STA/REPT/ST$_{B/F}$

She was concerned that the material might
be too easy or her presentation might be
too simple.//   CS/STA/REPT/ST$_C$

She's learned a great deal about working
with children, how to handle them and
build relationships with them; and she's
learned very well how to be a more
effective leader.//   CT/STA/EVAL/ST$_L$

Children. The general topic, Children, was used to organize any
information about a child or children taught by teachers or student
teachers in the elementary school. The topic includes general and
specific information about what children have learned, are learning, will
learn, and/or need to learn. It includes information about the behavior,
feelings, needs, interests, abilities, and achievements of a particular
child or group of children. It also includes information about the background of a child or group of children, such as: emotional, social, or
intellectual development and/or home, family, or community life of a child
or group of children. General and specific information about children is
classified by use of one category.[1]

Examples:

They know how to pick out a root word.

---

[1] The symbol used in coding data is CHIL.

They have had some work on these prefixes;
they know <u>superman</u>, <u>supermarket</u>, and
<u>superintendent</u>.//   CT/STA/REPT/CHIL

If he has never been used to going to
school//   CS/STA/REPT/CHIL

He's undisciplined.//   CT/STA/REPT/CHIL

Then he probably finds the restrictions
that you have to have in class unbelievable.// CS/COM/REPT/CHIL

    <u>Curriculum/Materials</u>. The general topic, Curriculum/Materials, was

used to organize any information about what is, was, or will be taught by

teachers and student teachers to children in the elementary school. It

was also used to organize any information about the materials which

teachers, student teachers, and/or supervisors of student teachers have

used, use, or will use in connection with planning for teaching children,

teaching children, and/or supervising student teachers. General and

specific information about curriculum and materials is classified by use

of two categories.[1]

    Examples:

What topic are you on in social studies
right now?//   CS/QUS/REPT/CUR

We're on Canada; we started on Canada today.
We just finished the background; the
Royalists are moving to Canada. We started
with the explorers, and now we're on Canada.// CT/STA/REPT/CUR

I think the science bulletins are simply
marvelous because they sketch out every
single thing that you need to do, very

---

    [1]The two categories and coding symbols are: Curriculum (CUR);
Materials (MAT).

```
        simple to follow.  They're about the best
        bulletins, curriculum bulletins, I've ever
        seen.//                                          CT/STA/EVAL/MAT
```

Situational Information. The general topic, Situational Information,

was used to organize any information about the school/community, college/

Preservice Program, and cooperating teacher/college supervisor personal

situations. General and specific information about these situations is

classified by use of three categories.[1]

Examples:

```
        While we were on probation we were observed
        twice a year, once by the vice principal
        and once by the principal; but the probation
        procedure has changed, and the principal had
        to observe everyone on probation before
        December.//                                      CS/STA/REPT/SCH


        We have a study at the college right now on
        this, on trying to abstract these particular
        elements so that the students can be helped
        to become aware of what they're saying and
        asking, so that they can decide, "Are those
        really the kinds of questions I wanted to
        ask, was that really the way I wanted to
        reject that particular idea.//                   CS/STA/REPT/COL


        When I was doing student teaching I was
        taking courses in the afternoons and
        evenings.  Preparing work for student
        teaching plus going to classes was quite
        a chore.//                                       CT/STA/REPT/CT-CSP
```

---

[1]The three categories and coding symbols are: School/Community
Situation (SCH); College/Preservice Program Situation (COL); Cooperating
Teacher/College Supervisor Personal (CT-CSP).

Summary of Quantitative Findings[1]

The report of the study presents and interprets: (1) frequency an~~d~~
percentage of units and lines devoted to each category or general topic
for categories in the three dimensions for all supervisory conferences
combined, (2) findings for categories or general topics and the amount of
student teacher difficulty for the six sets of conferences, and (3) frequency and percentage of units devoted to each category or general topic
by cooperating teachers and the college supervisor for all supervisory
conferences combined.

Supervisory Conferences

Examination of the number of units and lines, the amount of studen~~t~~
teacher difficulty, and the number of units and lines spoken by the
cooperating teacher and college supervisor for the six sets of conference~~s~~
revealed that the six sets of conferences varied with respect to amount o~~f~~
student teacher difficulty and number of units and lines. When the sets
of conferences were ranked and rank order correlations computed, correlations were found among Amount of Student Teacher Difficulty and Number of
Units and Lines. The correlations indicated that the number of units and
lines in these supervisory conferences increased with the amount of difficulty the student teacher was having.

Findings with regard to two groups of three conference sets

---

[1]For a complete discussion of the data see Theodora Randall Kimsey,
"The Work of One College Supervisor with Cooperating Teachers in Off-
Campus Schools: An Analysis of Conferences" (unpublished Ed.D. dissertation, Teachers College, Columbia University, New York, 1969), pp. 72-128,
156-220.

disclosed that the sets of conferences associated with students having less difficulty had, on the average, approximately three-fourths the number of units and lines as the sets of conferences associated with students having more difficulty. This suggested that the cooperating teachers and the college supervisor in these supervisory conferences had almost as much to discuss when the student teacher was having less difficulty as when the student teacher was having more difficulty. This conclusion is somewhat contrary to popular belief among, and a common practice for, many teacher educators, i.e., the cooperating teacher and college supervisor have little to discuss when the student teacher is not having serious difficulty; consequently, supervisory conferences between the two may be brief and take place infrequently.

Data pertaining to number and percentage of units and lines spoken by the cooperating teacher and the college supervisor for the six sets of conferences disclosed that percentages for the two speakers were markedly similar in most sets of conferences.

Interactive Dimension Categories

Data relating to Interactive Dimension categories for all supervisory conferences combined indicated that Stating accounted for a large proportion of units and lines while Reacting, Questioning, and Completing received relatively small proportions.[1] Nearly three-fourths of the units were devoted to Stating. This indicated that giving information was the

_____

[1]These findings for categories were supported by the data for the six sets of conferences; the sets of conferences were markedly similar with regard to the percentage of units and lines devoted to categories in the Interactive Dimension.

function served by most of the actions taken by speakers in these supervisory conferences. The ratio between Stating and Questioning actions, almost 9 to 1, indicated that most information was given voluntarily, i.e., by choice rather than as a response to a direct question.

Findings for the six sets of conferences disclosed that there was little or no correlation among Amount of Student Teacher Difficulty and the Percentage of Units and Lines in each Interactive Dimension category.

Data for all supervisory conferences combined revealed that cooperating teachers and the college supervisor devoted a large percentage of the units to Stating while devoting relatively small percentages to the other three categories. Although the talk of cooperating teachers and the college supervisor was similar with regard to the proportion of units devoted to categories in the Interactive Dimension, the college supervisor percentage in the category of Questioning was ten times that of cooperating teachers. The cooperating teacher percentage in Reacting was twice that of the college supervisor and in Stating one-sixth larger than that of the college supervisor.

That the talk of cooperating teachers and the college supervisor would be different had been anticipated for the following reasons. The work of the cooperating teacher in the classroom with the student teacher enabled her to obtain much information with regard to the student teacher behavior and the situation in which the student teacher was working as well as information with respect to her own supervisory behavior with the student teacher. This information was relevant to achievement of the five objectives of supervisory conferences; it was not only sought by the college supervisor but usually given voluntarily by the cooperating teacher.

In contrast, the work of the college supervisor with student teachers enabled her to obtain information with regard to the behavior of many student teachers and the situations in which they were working as well as information with respect to her own supervisory behavior with these student teachers. A small proportion of this information focused directly on the student teacher assigned to a particular cooperating teacher; therefore, little of it was sought by cooperating teachers and only that which seemed to be relevant to the achievement of objectives was imparted by the college supervisor.

Logical Dimension Categories

In regard to Logical Dimension categories, data for all supervisory conferences combined indicated that Reports accounted for a large propor-tion of units and lines while Plans, Evaluations, and Prescriptions received relatively small proportions.[1] Three-fifths of the units were devoted to Reports. This indicated that factual and analytical information about the world was of paramount importance in the achievement of objectives during these supervisory conferences. The preponderance of Reports seemed to be accounted for when this operation was considered not only as an operational end (performed in connection with subject matter in order to achieve objectives) but also as an operational means (per-formed in relation to--as a basis for--the performance of other operations).

Specifically, Reports were the primary operation performed in

_____

[1]Data for the six sets of conferences supported these findings; the sets of conferences were similar with regard to the percentage of units and lines devoted to categories in the Logical Dimension.

connection with subject matter falling under each of the six general topics in the Substantive Dimension. This suggested that the operation was often employed by supervisors in the achievement of two objectives: (1) keeping one another informed of the supervisory actions each had taken with the student teacher and (2) sharing professional information pertinent to supervision of student teachers. Analysis of protocols revealed that Evaluations, Prescriptions, and Plans were often preceded by Reports which did little more than identify the particular event, action, person, or state of affairs about which judgments or opinions were then stated. The following is an example:

> CS He asked the children, "How many of you
> care whether people tell lies about you?"
> Then he asked, "Can it be bad if people
> don't tell the truth about you?"//These   CS/STA/REPT/STTB$_L$
> were good questions, an improvement over
> the last time.//   CS/STA/EVAL/STTB$_L$

Thus, Reports were often a necessary preliminary to the performance of other operations which, in turn, were employed in the achievement of objectives.

Data pertaining to Plans indicated that the importance of this operation was considerable; approximately one-sixth of the units was devoted to this category. Plans were most often stated in connection with categories falling under the general topics of Teaching Behavior[1]

---

[1]Data relating to percentage of units devoted to each of the categories within the general topic, Teaching Behavior, disclosed that a large proportion (somewhat over two-thirds) of the talk was about various aspects of the student teacher's teaching behavior.

and Supervising Behavior.[1] These findings suggested that employment of
this operation by supervisors was primarily related to the achievement
of two objectives: (1) planning for the student teacher's future progress
with regard to becoming a teacher and (2) planning the supervisory actions
each would take with the student teacher.

Findings related to Evaluations and Prescriptions indicated that
the two operations, singly, accounted for a small proportion of the units
in these supervisory conferences (one-eighth and one-tenth, respectively).
Evaluations and Prescriptions were most often associated with categories
falling under the general topic of Teaching Behavior. Analysis of protocols revealed that evaluative statements were usually positive, almost
never negative; speakers often stated that something the student teacher
had done was "good" or "marvelous" but never stated that what the student
had done was "bad" or "terrible." Negative ratings of the student teacher
were usually given indirectly, implied in prescriptive statements, e.g.,
"That was too much for one lesson" and "If she had given more examples,
that would have helped." These findings seemed to indicate that Evaluations and Prescriptions were, in a way, the two sides of a single operation. Information about the subject matter with which Evaluations and
Prescriptions were usually associated and the way in which the two
operations were related suggested that the two operations were employed
in the achievement of a single objective, that is, determining the student

---

[1]Data for categories falling under Supervisory Behavior indicated
that a major proportion (almost nine-thenths) of the units was spent
discussing various aspects of the cooperating teacher's and college
supervisor's supervising behavior.

teacher's present status with respect to learning how to teach. When
the data related to Evaluations and Prescriptions were combined it was
found that the two operations accounted for somewhat over one-fifth of
the units in these supervisory conferences.

Findings for the six sets of conferences disclosed correlations
among Amount of Student Teacher Difficulty and the Percentage of Units in
Reports and the Percentage of Units and Lines in Prescriptions. These
correlations indicated: (1) the proportion of units devoted to Reports
decreased as the amount of difficulty the student teacher was having
increased and (2) the proportion of units and lines devoted to Prescriptions increased with the amount of difficulty the student teacher was
having. Nevertheless, it was believed that these correlations were somewhat misleading; variance in percentages relative to Reports and Prescriptions was not large and distribution of percentages in both categories
was uneven.

Data for all supervisory conferences combined revealed that the
talk of cooperating teachers and the college supervisor was very similar
with regard to the proportion of units devoted to categories in the Logical Dimension. Cooperating teachers and the college supervisor devoted a
large percentage of their units to Reports while devoting relatively small
percentages to the other three categories; however, the college supervisor
percentage in the category of Plans was almost one-fourth larger than that
of cooperating teachers.

Substantive Dimension General Topics

Data pertaining to Substantive Dimension general topics for all

198

supervisory conferences combined indicated: (1) Teaching Behavior accounted for a large proportion of units and lines; (2) Supervising Behavior, Student Teachers, and Children received relatively small proportions; and (3) Curriculum/Materials and Situational Information received very small proportions.[1]

Supervising Behavior, Teaching Behavior, and Student Teachers combined accounted for over three-fourths of the units in these supervisory conferences.[2] The predominance of these three topics was not unexpected because performance of operations in connection with subject matter within the three was necessary in order to achieve four of the objectives for supervisory conferences. Specifically, performance of operations in connection with various categories falling under Supervising Behavior was necessary in order that supervisors might: (1) keep one another informed of the supervisory actions each had taken with the student teacher and (2) plan the supervisory actions each would take with the student teacher. Performance of operations relative to various categories within Teaching Behavior and Student Teachers was necessary in order that supervisors might: (1) determine the student teacher's present status with respect to learning how to teach, and (2) plan for the student teacher's future progress with regard to becoming a teacher.

---

[1]These findings were supported by data for the six sets of conferences even though the sets of conferences were only fairly similar with regard to the percentage of units and lines devoted to general topics for categories in the Substantive Dimension.

[2]Supervising Behavior accounted for one-sixth of the units, Teaching Behavior somewhat less than one-half, and Student Teachers somewhat less than one-seventh.

Children, Curriculum/Materials, and Situational Information combine accounted for somewhat less than one-fourth of the units in these supervisory conferences.[1] The performance of operations in connection with these three topics seemed to be related, primarily, to the achievement of one objective, i.e., sharing professional information pertinent to the supervision of student teachers.

Findings for the six sets of conferences disclosed correlations among Amount of Student Teacher Difficulty and the Percentage of Units and Lines in Curriculum/Materials and the Percentage of Units and Lines in Supervising Behavior. The correlations suggested two relationships: (1) the proportion of units and lines devoted to Curriculum/Materials decreased as the amount of difficulty the student teacher was having increased and (2) the proportion of units and lines devoted to Supervising Behavior increased with the amount of difficulty the student teacher was having. Distribution of percentages in categories provided support for the first relationship but not the second; distribution of percentages relative to Supervising Behavior was uneven.

Data for all supervisory conferences combined indicated that the talk of cooperating teachers and the college supervisor was very similar with regard to the proportion of units devoted to general topics for categories in the Substantive Dimension. Cooperating teachers and the college supervisor devoted a large percentage of their units to Teaching Behavior, small percentages to Supervising Behavior, Student Teachers, and

---

[1]Children received somewhat less than one-seventh of the units, Curriculum/Materials just over one-twentieth, and Situational Information somewhat less than one-twentieth.

Children, and very small percentages to Curriculum/Materials and Situational Information. In regard to differences in percentages, the college supervisor percentage in the category of Supervising Behavior was almost one-third larger than that of cooperating teachers while the cooperating teacher percentage in Children was almost one-fourth larger than that of the college supervisor.

Implications of the Study

The study reported here is part of a larger research project on the behavior of supervisors of student teachers. Phase one of the project has been a series of studies to develop models for describing and analyzing the verbal behavior of college supervisors and cooperating teachers during supervisory conferences in order to produce empirically based instructional systems which can be used in further research directed toward, ultimately, improvement of the ability of supervisors to guide student teachers during the student teaching period.

Implications for Future Research

No research directed toward improvement of student teacher supervision can disregard the relationship between the college supervisor and cooperating teacher. The relationship affects the supervisory practices of each with the student teacher. The present study has provided information which could prove productive in terms of greater understanding of this relationship.

The system of analysis identifies variables of supervisory conferences between the college supervisor and the cooperating teacher.

Knowledge about these variables will be useful in the construction of empirically based instructional systems which can be used in further research on the behavior of college supervisors and cooperating teachers. It will enable future researchers to postulate hypotheses concerning the relationship between the verbal interaction of supervisors with one another and their subsequent behavior with student teachers and, further, the effect of this on student teachers, their behavior with pupils in the classroom.

Future researchers should give attention to verification and/or modification of the system of analysis developed in this study. The category system was developed, tested, and applied through use of data for the supervisory conferences of one college supervisor with six cooperating teachers. Therefore, it is recommended that the system of analysis be tested and applied to data for a less limited population.

The report of quantitative findings suggests interrelationships among categories in the several dimensions and the occurrence of these in sequential patterns. Future studies might be directed toward determining not only the interrelationships among categories but those patterns of interaction which are most effective in achievement of the objectives for supervisory conferences.

As constructed, the system of analysis cannot be used to identify the beginning and/or end of cycles, that is, talk directed toward the achievement of a specific objective. Study of protocols revealed, however, that some Stating and Questioning actions were initiators of cycles while others were continuants. Further refinement of Interactive Dimension categories would enable researchers to identify those actions which

202

initiated cycles of behavior and the role of the college supervisor and cooperating teacher in the initiation of these.

Implications for the Preparation and Training of Supervisors

The system of analysis, used as an analytic tool, can be an aid in the preparation and training of college supervisors and cooperating teachers. It can help prospective supervisors and/or practitioners already in the field to become aware of their behavior in supervisory conferences. An objective analysis of the behavior in supervisory conferences can be of use to supervisors and prospective supervisors in the development of more effective conferring behaviors.

Interpretation of quantitative findings in terms of functions served or objectives of supervisory conferences can also be useful in the preparation and training of supervisors. By providing needed information as to the ways and means of working together as a supervisory team, it can help practitioners and prospective supervisors alike gain some insight into major problems confronting teacher educators today, that is, the development of effective cooperative relations between schools and colleges engaged in teacher education and the development of innovative partnership approaches in the supervision of student teachers by cooperating teachers and college supervisors. Factual information about how and on what the college supervisor and cooperating teacher work cooperatively with one another and how they coordinate their work with regard to the separate actions taken by each with the student teacher might prompt the trainee to develop guidelines for effective conduct of supervisory conferences.

Implications for Inservice Training of Cooperating Teachers by
the College Supervisor

The importance of the cooperating teacher in the preparation of
teachers is inestimable. Educational research provides evidence which
seems to indicate that the cooperating teacher has a greater influence on
the prospective teacher than other educators in the professional sequence.
Nevertheless, many teacher educators believe that "the weakest part of
the teacher education program is the 'supervising' teacher."[1] They believe
that cooperating teachers need special preparation and/or continued help if
they are to provide student teaching experiences of high quality.

Helping the cooperating teacher provide high quality student teaching experiences is recognized as one of the major functions of the college
supervisor. If the college supervisor has an obligation to provide not
only the help which many cooperating teachers need in order to provide
high quality student teaching experiences but inservice training for
cooperating teachers as well, then the supervisory conference of the college supervisor with the cooperating teacher is an excellent opportunity
for the college supervisor to supply this help and inservice training.

It is the belief of the investigators involved in the series of
studies reported in this monograph that those persons designated as college supervisors of student teachers need to re-examine their roles and
functions. Classroom teachers working with student teachers have more

---

[1]A. R. Mead, "A Symposium on Teacher Education," *Journal of Teacher
Education*, 14:37, March, 1963.

continuous and intimate contact with their students than do college supervisors with the same students. Based on this fact, it is proposed that college supervisors might better devote their time and energies to working directly with cooperating teachers in helping them to improve their competence in guidance of student teachers. Hence, college supervisors might make their best contribution to the quality of student teachers' experiences by working through those who have daily contact with them and opportunities in abundance to assist novices in their becoming professional performers.

This study of one college supervisor working with six cooperating teachers may serve as a base for examination of the nature of the contribution made by the supervisor and for projections as to how that supervisor might work, if the task were to provide help for the cooperating teacher rather than to focus on specific student teachers most of the time. It is likely that the kind of general help the college supervisor provides could be offered in group seminar and laboratory type situations, rather than solely in dyadic conferences.

Supervision of student teaching is an expensive component of university programs. If ways and means can be found for extending the contributions of university personnel, cost of the program may be ameliorated to some degree. Much study is needed to develop new conceptions of roles and functions of college supervisors. Meanwhile, if college supervisors are going to continue their practice of observing student teachers at work and then conferring with cooperating teachers about the work of the students, the present study is highly useful in suggesting ways of examining behavior of the two partners--college supervisor and cooperating teacher.

Chapter VII

THE COLLEGE SUPERVISOR AS SEMINAR TEACHER
Norma Mertz

The growing interest in the study of teaching as an approach to the
preparation of teachers is reflected in a number of professional education
curricula. In a few preparatory institutions teacher education curricula
focused on the study of teaching have replaced former programs or now
parallel existing programs. In other institutions one or more courses in
the existing professional sequence have been revised or replaced by
courses directed to the study of teaching.

These curricular changes and the general interest in this and like
conceptual approaches to the preparation of teachers raise questions about
the personnel who are to guide pre- and in-service professional in the
study of teaching. Who is to guide the novice in the study of teaching?
What role(s) is he to play? What responsibilities does he have? How is
he to proceed in the various settings in which teaching is to be studied?
Other chapters in this monograph discuss these questions as they pertain
to a variety of conference arrangements involving different groupings of
supervisors who guide students in the study of teaching. This chapter
examines the college supervisor as teacher of classes and seminars
directed to the study of teaching.

The first section of the chapter examines the study of teaching as pursued by groups of students in classes and seminars, the teachers of such courses, and the college supervisor. In the second section reports of two current studies which look at the work of college supervisors in guiding groups of students are presented. In the third section the implications of these studies for the college supervisor as teacher of such groups are related to the questions raised about the personnel who are to guide others in the study of teaching.

The Study of Teaching in Courses and Seminars

It is not known how many institutions offer or are planning courses and programs directed to the study of teaching. Many of the offerings that can be identified are in the early, experimental and developmental stages. A few of them have been detailed in the professional literature, but many of them have either not yet been reported or been reported in less detail than might be desired. It is difficult and perhaps misleading to attempt to abstract a general description of these efforts at this time, but exploration of teacher behavior in courses directed to the study of teaching makes it necessary.

The Course

The number of courses directed to the study of teaching within a given preparatory curriculum, the placement of a course or courses, and the precise nature and content of the course(s) vary from one program to another. Some commonalities, though, appear to exist. Each of the courses requires laboratory-type experiences as an integral part or an intimate adjunct to it. Often a sequence of real and vicarious experiences is followed by an intensive laboratory experience, e.g., student teaching. The coursework is closely tied in with the experiential component in the laboratory. The coursework prepares the student for systematically analyzing the experiences and uses the experiences as source material in the course.

All of the courses teach the student one or more classificatory and analytical techniques for gathering and analyzing objective data. The student is trained to use the technique(s) and, in some programs, a model or models of teaching and/or conceptual system(s) for observing and analyzing teaching behavior. These may be presented to him or developed by him. Usually the novice is expected to use some systematic approach to recording and analyzing his own teaching as a final step in the training process.

Several programs involve directing or redirecting the student's teaching behavior in accordance with the models studied, the value positions inherent in the classification scheme or conceptual system taught, or into a "personally satisfying" teaching style. One must note that where this is a facet of the program it is in marked contrast to the directing and redirecting commonly associated with education courses. In all of the programs in which it appears, whether or not there is to be a redirection and, if there is to be, the nature and direction of such change is a determination of the student, himself, not the teacher.

Most of the courses involve instructional sessions--to teach the techniques, models or systems involved, practice sessions--to insure competence in the use of these as well as to provide opportunities for trying alternate teaching patterns, and group sessions--to discuss analyzed experiences and proposed teaching behaviors. Generally these methods are interwoven in the course and the definitional and traditional distinctions between seminars and classes are erased.

In objectives, the courses are strikingly congruous. They attempt to provide the prospective professional with the tools, one or several, for gathering and analyzing objective data about teaching and teaching behavior; they encourage a student to conceptualize goals he can and hopefully will use to examine and control his own teaching patterns in service. They strive to produce a professional who, once methodologically armed, will continue to be a student of teaching and a researcher in teaching throughout his teaching career. They seek to expose the student to teaching and the practice of teaching in all of its dimensions. Underlying and activating these objectives is an assumption that is widely accepted in the profession, but little practiced in traditional programs: one learns to do by doing, and to be by being.

A glimpse of selected offerings lends substance to this abstracted description and illustrates something of the nature and direction of some current experiments. In selecting specific courses or programs there has been no attempt to be inclusive or to select those which might be most representative or well known.[1]

---

[1] For a more extensive description of some current offerings, see: Father Edward Hancko, "Influence of Descriptive Studies of Teaching Behavior on the Preservice Professional Preparation of Teachers" (unpublished Ed.D. dissertation, Teachers College, Columbia University, 1968); and "Part III Action Programs," The Study of Teaching, Dean Corrigan, ed. (Washington, D.C.: AST, 1967), pp. 33-63.

In a general methods course offered to prospective
secondary school teachers at Ohio State University,
students are taught to categorize and analyze classroom
verbal behavior using Flanders' System of Interaction
Analysis, as modified by Hough and Ober, so that they
may possess a "tool for instructional self-improvement."
As part of the work of the course the student is required
to prepare and teach a video-taped lesson to his peers.
The "class" provides the "teacher" with immediate feedback and subsequently plots the lesson on the Flanders
Matrix. The "teacher" is asked to objectively evaluate
his teaching performance, taking into account his pre-
stated objectives, the feedback from the "class," and
data from a matrix he prepared for himself from a review
of the tape of the lesson.[1]

Stanford University offers clinics for pre-service
teachers in which they may attain and practice the nine
technical skills which have been identified and taught
to them as the component acts of teaching. At the outset
the student presents a ten-minute lesson. The video-taped
lesson is diagnosed within the framework of the skills and
a specific program is prepared to assist the student in
attaining the skills he lacks or in which he is weak.
Subsequently the student prepares and presents a series
of five minute lessons to four or five children whose
behavior is predetermined to direct the "teacher's" attention and responses to the particular skill being developed.
The video-tape of each lesson is observed by the student
by means of a prepared guide and skill-rating form developed
at Stanford. The student then views a video-tape of a
teacher whose performance in that area is deemed sound, and
he attempts to compare his behavior with that of the model
and to evolve ways in which he might further improve his
skill.[2]

"The Better Teaching Project," conceived and directed
by Charles Galloway and Robert Strom, is an in-service
program offered to teachers in the Hough District of

---

[1]This description was taken from a preliminary report prepared by
Father Edward Hancko from materials and interviews he collected at the
School of Education, Ohio State University, in October, 1966, in the
preparation of his dissertation. Hancko, loc. cit.

[2]This description was evolved from a preliminary report prepared
by Father Edward Hancko from interviews with professional personnel at
the School of Education, Stanford University in November, 1966, in the
preparation of his dissertation. Hancko, loc. cit.

Cleveland by Ohio State University. The aim of the program is to help each teacher enunciate his goals and determine whether or not he is actualizing them. The teacher is helped to specify his particular intentions and to state the conditions under which they may occur. An assessment is then made to determine whether these intentions are being actualized. A coding system, developed for the assessment, is used to prepare objective descriptions of the teacher's behavior and the students' responses in the classroom. The teacher is taught to prepare and use these descriptions as well. The teacher completes a specially designed inventory to explore his assessment of his success in actualizing his intentions and his students complete a rating form on his performance. In addition, tests are administered to the teacher to reveal his "selfhood." The teacher and the help-agent use the results of these instruments to determine whether or not the teacher's intentions are actualized in his behavior. Where they are not, they plan ways in which these goals might be actualized, and, after the teacher tries them, further data are collected to determine the teacher's success using new approaches.[1]

An experimental curriculum, wholly directed to the study of teaching and the practice of what is studied, is offered to prospective elementary school teachers at Hofstra University, Hempstead, New York. The course and interrelated experiences are intended to structure the student's view and practice of teaching.

The first two courses in the sequence are directed to the study of the child, his affective and cognitive development, and to learning to gather and organize observational data. Students are taught to produce descriptive observational reports, without subjective comment, to use an observational schedule concerned with "coping behavior" developed by Ruth Formanek and Robert Spaulding, to apply the cognitive objectives enumerated by Bloom in his Taxonomy of Educational Objectives, and to administer Piagetian tests. These instruments are applied to films of selected aspects of child behavior, produced for the program, to observation of children in different settings, and to the tutoring in which each student engages.

In the third and fourth courses in the sequence the students are trained to use the Aschner-Gallagher Category System, in order to examine the verbal behavior of teachers. The students use and practice this analytical system in and

---

[1]The program was described by Robert D. Strom and Charles Galloway, "Becoming a Better Teacher," The Journal of Teacher Education, 18:285-292, fall, 1967.

on their courses and teachers and in their teaching experience
with a small group of children. In each of the first four courses
the students study the "structure" of one of the disciplines
in an elementary school curriculum: social studies, language
arts, science and mathematics, and in the third and fourth
courses they study "discovery teaching." They prepare units
and materials relevant to the teaching of these disciplines
and practice using discovery methods in their teaching experience.

In the final two courses of the sequence, one of which
might be termed student teaching, the student is expected to
continue to learn and practice teaching discovery lessons,
to try a variety of teaching styles, to learn to deal with
the routines and demands of the classroom, and to gather
and analyze data concerning his own teaching behavior. From
observational descriptions, with which he has had previous
experience, the student is led to a categorization system
developed by Robert Spaulding by means of which the flow
of verbal interaction may be coded. A modified version of
the Aschner-Gallagher System is reintroduced, to provide
for the content of verbal interaction, and Bloom's cognitive
categories are reviewed. The student is then expected to
analyze his lessons, as prepared and presented in his student
teaching experience, using all of the objective data he can
amass and analytical tools he has learned.[1]

The Teacher

To date, there are no discussions in the professional literature
about the teacher of courses directed to the study of teaching. None of
the reported programs and courses deal directly with the questions of who
is teaching the course, what he is doing, or how, if at all, he was prepared for this teaching. Some inferences may be made from the descriptions and discussions of reported courses. The teacher must know and be
able to train others in the use of at least one technique or means of
gathering and analyzing objective data. In several of the programs he

---

[1]This description is derived from a mimeographed bulletin prepared
for the AERA Conference, February 10, 1968. Constant Madon, Harold
Morine, Charles Swenson, Ruth Formanek, Selma Greenburg, and Greta Morine,
"A Symposium: An Experimental Curriculum for Teacher Training," Hofstra
University.

must know a variety of techniques and a range of conceptual models and systems for studying teaching, and it is probably safe to suggest that he must know and be able to use all of the techniques and models that might be applicable. As systems are modified and/or new systems emerge, he must be prepared to retrain himself and restructure his course of training.

The teacher must have intimate knowledge of teaching, as it is practiced and as it might be practiced, and of schools. He must be able to provide the student with objective feedback about teaching performance, the student's if it is observed or others', in the same "language," i.e., classificatory and analytical scheme, as taught to and used by the student.[1] He must help the student to see the relevance of the techniques, models, or systems taught to the work of the teacher and assist him in using them for the examination and control of his teaching behavior. He must aid the students in stating their goals explicitly and testing their actualization,[2] and in identifying and trying alternative teaching behaviors to those they have exhibited or observed.[3]

The teacher questions and clarifies what is said and written by students, individually and in groups, and encourages them to question themselves and each other. The teacher does not judge the student's practice of teaching. He assists the student in investigating his own practice of teaching and that done by others but leaves the valuing process

---

[1]As suggested by Strom and Galloway, loc. cit.

[2]Ibid.

[3]As inferred from Edmund J. Amidon, "The Use of Interaction Analysis at Temple University," The Study of Teaching, Dean Corrigan, ed. (Washington, D.C.: AST, 1967), pp. 42-54.

and decisions to change to the student. He is available to assist the student in making changes in his behavior, if the student wishes to make such changes, and he is alert to possibilities of judgments being made upon erroneous data or faulty assumptions.

Amidon suggests that students often feel threatened when they attempt to observe and analyze and perhaps change their teaching behavior.[1] Their teachers need to provide and maintain a supportive atmosphere and be ready to reduce the levels of threat felt by individual students.

Implied in the descriptions of courses directed to the study of teaching is the notion that the teacher of such courses must be a model of the teacher he wishes the prospective teacher to become; that he must be engaged in the study of his own teaching behavior, and he must actualize the objectives of the course.

The College Supervisor

The title, college supervisor, is a functional designation for a member of the college faculty who guides and directs pre-service students in professional laboratory experiences as part or all of his university teaching responsibilities. The work of the college supervisor has been much discussed and investigated in the professional literature and the position itself has become common to almost all teacher preparatory programs. The college supervisor often selects and places the prospective teacher in a particular laboratory experience, most commonly student teaching, selects

---

[1]Edmund J. Amidon and Evan Powell, "Interaction Analysis of a Feedback System in Teacher Preparation," The Supervisor: Agent for Change in Teaching, James Raths and Robert Leeper, eds. (Washington, D.C.: ASCD, 1966), p. 55.

214

the classroom teacher with or under whom he will work, makes the university objectives for requiring the experience and its expectations of the student teacher and cooperating teacher explicit, periodically visits the student teacher in the situation and meets with him for conferences about his experience and his teaching performance as observed, and talks with the cooperating teacher about the student teacher's progress and the nature of the experience being provided for him.

In previous chapters modifications in the approach to the supervision of pre-professionals have been suggested. The emerging pattern requires the college supervisor to provide the pre-professional with objective feedback for himself, and to assist him in analyzing this data and comparing it with desired or desirable teaching behavior. Together, the supervisor and pre-professional engage in the study of teaching as performed by the student.

The college supervisor often conducts seminars with groups of students concurrently engaged in laboratory experiences. The seminar may be a formal course requirement or an informal dimension of the laboratory experience. The college supervisor may conduct a seminar with students he supervises or with ones he does not supervise, depending upon the program and policies of the institution.

Seminars, as companions to laboratory experiences, have a long history in teacher education, but surprisingly, very little has been written describing or prescribing the nature, content, and conduct of such seminars. Traditionally, seminar appears to be a time and place for the "agonies and ecstasies" of the concurrent laboratory experience, as perceived by the student teacher, to be related by him and dissected by the group and/or seminar leader. The students' specific problems and concerns are presented in the seminar and the group and/or leader seek and evaluate prescriptions for action.

In many preparatory programs the laboratory experience is the prospective teacher's first experience in the role of a teacher in a classroom situation, and the experience and seminar come at the end of the program, having been preceded by a number of courses in which theoretical and foundational understandings have been presented. In these cases the seminar is intended to help students to integrate the theory and practice of teaching. In addition, the seminar may deal with a variety of professional concerns and dimensions, e.g., how to get a job, professional organizations.

Changes are occurring in these seminars. While continuing the supportive and "therapeutic" functions, the idea that a teacher can and should observe and analyze his teaching behavior is being introduced and stressed in a good many seminars. The pre-professional is being asked and helped to describe objectively what happened in a particular situation and is assisted in analyzing his actions, and those of others in the group, by the seminar leader. Instead of seeking or offering prescriptions for behavior the seminar leader guides students in making their own decisions through comparing analyses of their behavior and its effects with their desires and perceptions of teaching. The seminar teacher prods the student to state, clarify, and justify their desires and perceptions so that they can be actualized. In some instances techniques for analyzing behavior are taught and/or models and systems presented or developed.

If the parallels between the work of the college supervisor in emerging seminars, as well as in the supervision of pre-professionals in laboratory experiences, and the inferred work of teachers in classes and seminars directed to the study of teaching in emerging teacher preparation programs are striking, it is worth noting that the trends are inextricably interrelated. They are part and parcel of the changes in thinking and in approach to the preparation of teachers, now conceived of more as a single, on-going process rather than a collection of discrete courses or experiences.

The College Supervisor as Teacher: Two Studies

The number of studies directed to and emanating from a focus on the study of teaching is increasing, as is suggested by the studies included in this monograph. Studies recently completed or currently underway include attempts (1) to modify, adapt, or interrelate existing schema for collecting and analyzing objective data; (2) to develop "new" classificatory systems and to use such systems to analyze teaching; (3) to construct courses or programs of teacher training which focus on the study of teaching and train prospective teachers to use such systems; or (4) to explore the impact and implications of this kind of research on teaching.

The two studies presented here are illustrative. More importantly for the purposes of this chapter, they direct attention to the college supervisor as teacher and to the implications of the current focus and interest in the study of teaching for teacher educators. In a study

recently completed, Hill[1] examined the verbal behavior of teachers and
their students during nursing seminars. Using a variety of established
analytical schemes, she documents the intimate relationship between the
level of the teacher's thinking, as expressed in his verbal discourse in
the classroom, and that of the students, as similarly expressed. According to Hill, her findings strongly recommend the study of verbal behavior,
the teacher's and the students', in the preparation of teachers and as a
continuing responsibility in service. In a study currently underway the
writer attempted to train prospective teachers to use the natural history
method as a means for studying their own practice of teaching. In describing and analyzing the training program and the results of it, questions
are raised about the method and its potential for the study of teaching
by preservice students.

A Study of the Verbal Interaction Between Master Teachers and Students During Clinical Nursing Conferences[2]

The purpose of the study was to describe and analyze the verbal
behavior of teachers and students to determine what relationships, if
any, appeared to exist between the verbal behavior of the teacher and
levels of thinking by the students. Although the social and emotional
climate of the classroom admittedly affects the learning process, the
study considered only the levels of thinking expressed verbally during

---

[1] Jean Hill, "A Study of Verbal Interaction Between Master Teachers
and Students During Clinical Nursing Conferences" (Ed.D. dissertation,
Teachers College, Columbia University, 1968).

[2] This review was prepared by Jean Hill, the author of the study.

218

clinical conferences concerned with the nursing care of children.

Ten college teachers in fully-accredited baccalaureate nursing programs were asked to submit tape recordings of three clinical nursing conferences held in sequence. The teachers selected were considered to be "master teachers" in terms of experience, preparation, and reputation. They were asked to conduct the conferences in their usual manner as recordings of typical verbal interaction were desired for a descriptive study. Students were told the purpose of the tape recording. No observer was present during the conferences.

A total of twenty-eight tape recorded conferences was submitted. Three sets of conferences were disqualified and two teachers submitted only two conferences each due to mechanical difficulties in recording. Therefore, the data consisted of verbatim transcriptions of nineteen tape recorded clinical nursing conferences held by seven teachers. The students involved were sophomores in two schools, juniors in four schools and seniors in one school. There were four to seven students in each conference group.

All conferences in the study were held for a minimum of one hour and were related to the current experience and nursing problems of the students. The setting of the clinical nursing conference was chosen because case conferences have been considered to be particularly valuable media for the development of professional judgment. Conferences provide an opportunity for students to analyze nursing practice and to develop or discover principles and concepts which may be tested in new situations. The clinical conference should provide a supervised, systematic exercise in a diagnosis of a problem, organization of data, selection and testing

219

of hypotheses, and development of a way of thinking which is professionally productive. A secondary purpose of some conferences seems to be to facilitate vicarious learning through sharing of experiences and observations.

System of Analysis

The protocols were analyzed by a multidimensional code to identify the units of discourse, the pedagogic functions performed, and the level of thinking expressed by the utterances of teachers and students. Flow charts were developed to clarify the patterns of interaction and the relationships between the levels of thinking expressed in the discourse. Identification of the variety and frequency of use of different teaching cycles indicated the flexibility of teaching style. A modified interaction analysis matrix was used to present graphically the relationship between the level of thinking expressed in the teacher's solicitations and the students' responses. Calculations were made of the percentages of all utterances at the different levels of thinking for the teacher and for the students during each conference. The summaries were presented in charts.

The first step in analysis was to divide the protocols into units within which relationships between utterances of teachers and students might be sought. Rather than divide the protocols into arbitrary time units, the discourse was divided into segments each of which seemed concerned with one content objective or one aspect of a nursing problem. Segments were called "thought units" and were identified by use of criteria adapted from Smith[1] (unit deals with a single topic or a single content objective and includes all the contiguous discourse relevant to the topic).

Thought units varied in length from two or three exchanges to several pages of protocol. A variety of related elements such as facts, definitions, comparisons, or generalizations were sometimes included in a single thought unit. While content objectives might not be covertly stated, it was usually possible to identify one key idea or concept around which the discourse within the unit was organized.

Once the thought units had been identified, the pedagogic function which each utterance served was indicated using criteria developed by Bellack and Davitz, et al.[2] Pedagogic moves are basically of two types: initiatory moves of structuring and soliciting, used to introduce the discussion and to elicit a verbal response, and reflexive moves of responding, which bear a reciprocal relationship to the initiatory move of soliciting and reflexive moves of reacting, which serve to modify or to expand the discourse.

Cognitive categories for classifying utterances into four levels of thinking were developed from the Taxonomy of Educational Objectives.[3] The

---

[1]B. Othanel Smith, et al., A Tentative Report on the Strategies of Teaching (Urbana, Illinois: Bureau of Research, College of Education, University of Illinois, 1964), pp. 12-15.

[2]Arno A. Bellack and Joel Davitz, et al., The Language of the Classroom (New York: Institute of Psychological Research, Teachers College, Columbia University, 1963).

[3]Benjamin S. Bloom (ed.), Taxonomy of Educational Objectives: Handbook I. Cognitive Domain (New York: Longmans, Green and Co., 1956).

hierarchical ordering of the categories was unidirectional with each successive step dependent upon mastery of the preceding steps. In categorizing the level of thinking verbalized in a soliciting move, the level
of thinking logically called for in the response was considered rather
than the level actually elicited. The cognitive categories were, briefly:
Step A--Recall, Recognize, Report or State; Step B--Describe, Define,
Classify, Compare, Contrast, Opine; Step C--Apply, Infer, Explain,
Generalize; Step D--Analyze, Evaluate, Judge, Synthesize; Non-Cognitive
Utterances; and Non-Codable Utterances.

The use of the multidimensional code made it possible to depict the
ebb and flow of the interaction between the teacher and student or students,
and the successive levels of thinking verbalized. The objectivity of
coding, however, seemed to be improved by stating the function served by
the utterance rather than the words spoken. The compact form or flow
chart resulting from the maneuver seemed to clarify both the teaching
style and the relationship between the verbal behavior of the teacher and
students. The flow chart also reduced the temptation of the coder to
identify with the teacher or to concentrate on the content of the
utterances.

Bellack's concept of teaching cycles was adopted to describe the
patterns of pedagogic moves used by teachers and students. Teaching style
included also the frequency and length of the utterances and the number of
students involved in one verbal interaction.

To present visually the possible relationship between the way in
which the teacher asked questions and the levels of thinking expressed by
students, a modified interaction analysis matrix was used. On the matrix,

222

the immediate responding move of the student to the soliciting move of the teacher was tabulated. The completed matrix represented visually the interactions between teacher and students, but not between students, and only soliciting and responding moves were considered.

Of equal concern was the total interaction for each level of thinking expressed during the conference. Therefore, the percentage of utterances at each level was calculated separately for teacher and students during each conference and reported in tables.

Findings of the Study

The length of the thought units varied between teachers and within conferences. One teacher organized the discourse around two broad content objectives in the first recorded conference and around four in the second and third. In contrast, in a conference of approximately the same length, another teacher used eight thought units. This factor may be related to individual teaching style since generally the number of units remained relatively stable for each teacher.

There appeared to be only moderate consistency in the teacher's use of any one teaching cycle within or between conferences. Although the teaching cycle of solicitation-response was frequently used, it was often modified by either multiple responding or reacting moves, or by both.

In terms of pedagogic moves, the college teachers of nursing observed the rules of the "teaching game." The use of structuring and soliciting moves was primarily the realm of the teacher, although students occasionally used both. Three teachers consistently used structuring

223

moves to establish the focus, to set the dimensions for the conference, and to determine the thought units within the conference. As would be expected, when conferences were used primarily for exchange or sharing of experiences rather than for evaluation or analysis of the experiences the teacher did little or no structuring. Students occasionally used structuring moves to introduce a topic, implying but not stating an invitation to participate. When a soliciting move followed such a structuring one, it was made by the teacher rather than by the student. Student-initiated thought units tended to be brief, unless the teacher assumed sponsorship.

Although some collegiate nursing students used soliciting moves freely, in only two protocols did they approximate the number of soliciting moves made by the teacher. In one such conference, a student assumed a teaching role for a portion of the period. The majority of soliciting moves by either teacher or student were made for actual information; only one-third of the moves were concerned with explanation or evaluation.

Responding moves appeared to be the exclusive domain of the student. Teachers rarely used the move, expecting students to answer student solicitations.

The use of the reacting move was shared. Students used it freely to extend or modify the interaction; teachers used reacting moves to elaborate ideas, to reiterate student responses, and to commend or express approval. While the use of approval varied from teacher to teacher, in conferences in which the teacher frequently commended the students, the latter expressed agreement with or approved utterances of both teacher and classmates. Students voiced opinions, compared experiences, or summarized

the discourse freely. In terms of frequency of use, students used reacting moves more often than did the teachers.

In total verbal activity, the college students in nursing equalled
or excelled the teacher in the frequency and length of their utterances.
The multiple responding and reacting moves typically made to one soliciting move of the teacher suggested that students expected to be involved.
The approval and agreement expressed seemed further evidence of the extent
of such involvement in their own learning.

Inspection of the interaction analysis matrices showed a positive
and close relationship between the verbal soliciting behavior of the
teacher and the responding moves of the students. In general, the students were at least twice as likely to respond at the level of the
teacher's soliciting move as at any other level. In those instances where
the response was not at the same level of thinking as the solicitation,
the tendency was for the student to respond in kind, but at a lower level.
For example, if evaluation was requested, the student might respond with
evaluation or express an opinion, but would rarely respond with analysis
or description.

When calculations were made separately of the percentages of discourse at the different levels of thinking during each conference, a close
and direct relationship between the verbal behavior of the teacher and the
student was demonstrated. The percentages of thinking expressed at the
different levels varied among conferences conducted by the same teacher
and among teachers. However, in conferences in which a high percentage of
the discourse of the teacher involved explanations or evaluation, a high
percentage of the discourse of students also was expressed at this level.

225

If the teacher's discourse expressed a high percentage of thinking at the level of factual recall or description, the discourse of the students also tended to remain at this level. From the data, it was evident that the teacher set the model for the level of thinking practiced by the students.

Soliciting moves which elicited expression of thinking at the upper levels logically required reasoning or encouraged divergent thinking. The nature of the question itself seemed to determine the level of thinking in the response. The evidence of this study indicated the vital importance of the way in which teachers ask questions. The focus and the dimensions of the classroom discourse were set by the questions posed by the teacher. If she requested a factual response, students gave one; when she asked that an inference or explanation be made, it was attempted. Through structuring and soliciting moves the teacher selected the facts of a problem for discussion and indicated the direction and the depth of thinking required or acceptable in the response.

Teachers differed in the way in which they paced the challenge to the different levels of thinking. Some teachers permitted or planned for eight or more interactions devoted to collection of factual data before soliciting for inferences from these data or for analysis of situations or modes of intervention. Others tended to move the discussions more rapidly to the level of inference or explanation or evaluation. How much of the difference was a function of the teaching strategy and how much might have been due to the content of the subject matter under discussion was not studied.

It appeared that within the conferences in which students expressed thinking above the level of recall (Step A) or opinion (Step B), teachers tended to establish the focus sharply and set the dimensions of the conference discussion. Within the thought units such teachers tended to proceed as follows:

1. They provided clues to pertinent data to be considered either in subject matter, experiences, or observations. Such clues appear to contribute to the clarity of student perception of the problem and of the appropriate method to be used. To the extent that the process of ordering pertinent data for problem solving becomes habitual, students learn a method of inquiry that is unique to the particular field of knowledge and develop resources for continuing self-learning.

2. They clarified through seeking definitions. Thinking involved a process of progressive discrimination between observable phenomena. Practice would facilitate development of this intellectual skill for present and future use.

3. They employed a strategy of teaching which moved from soliciting for a level of factual recall, through description, to application, or explanation, to analysis and evaluation before returning to the level of recall for further data. One measure of mastery in the teaching process seems to be the ability to vary the pace of demand for use of the higher mental processes of thinking in terms of the ability of the learner to respond appropriately. Undoubtedly both sequence and pace of demand influence the level of thinking in the learner.

4. They summarized or generalized the discourse near the end of a thought unit. If students are to become self-directed learners, development of the ability to transfer learning from a known to a new situation is an important skill. Both retention and transfer seem to be improved by reducing specifics to generalizations and such abstractions apparently are best learned in relationship to concrete phenomena.

5. They used verbal approval freely, either directly or indirectly. Acceptance of verbal participation by the learner appears to be associated with acceptance of the worth of the learner as a person. Frequent expressions of agreement with or approval of contributions of the students seem to create a climate in which students feel free to participate.

6. They encouraged participation as inferred from the use of multiple responding and reacting moves associated with

one soliciting move.

7. They provided immediate guidance through frequent interactions. Knowledge of the results seems to increase
   motivation for learning.

8. They used soliciting moves which were open-ended or were
   variations of the logical form, "If X, then Y." Students
   were challenged to use recalled information in thinking.
   At times inferences were solicited when there was not a
   "correct answer." If students are to learn to think logically or critically or creatively, then opportunities and
   guidance are needed for practice of this behavior.

Implications of the Study

The findings of the study seem to have implications for the improve-

ment of programs in nursing education at the graduate level and for the

in-service education of present faculty in schools of nursing.

The pre-service preparation of college teachers of nursing is of

vital concern to the future welfare of society. Teachers are needed for

new schools and for replacement and augmentation of faculty in established

schools. If Smith's supposition is accepted that much of the beginning

teacher's difficulty with instruction is due to his inability to handle

the verbal operations of teaching, then it would seem logical that pro-

grams preparing teachers would provide experiences specifically designed

to develop such verbal skills.

One means of strengthening the present pre-service experience

might be to give students practice in analyzing their own teaching by use

of the multidimensional code with tapescripts of their classes. A few

experiences in teaching, carefully analyzed for ways of asking questions

which elicit expressions of intellectual abilities and skills might be

more productive of effective verbal teaching behavior than more frequent but unexamined experiences. A further advantage of practice in analysis might lie in improving the ability of the student to conceptualize teaching. The system of analysis would provide the student with a tool for self-evaluation; a means for comparing the effects of different kinds of questions on the level of student thinking. Using with a group of students, analysis of tapescripts might be helpful in promoting learning through vicarious involvement. Teachers need to develop the habit of thinking critically and constructively about their own verbal behavior, and practice in self-analysis with an objective code would be one aid in so doing.

The findings seem to have relevance also for the improvement of supervision of practice teaching. When the supervising teacher directly observes teaching behavior as it occurs in the classroom, one act of instruction or response may unduly influence evaluation. One incident may cast a halo effect over the total observed behavior. Objective analysis of a verbatim transcription of verbal teaching-learning interaction would reduce the subjective elements of judgment and hence assist the supervising teacher to develop the skills and competencies needed for effective guidance of student teaching. A tapescript of the classroom interaction would relieve the college supervisor of the need always to be physically present. Because of the geographic separation of the classrooms in which students have teaching practice and the graduate school, the use of tapescripts would reduce both the time and cost of supervision.

A tapescript or protocol of teaching sessions, combined with an observation by closed circuit television or a kinescopic tape, would be a valuable source of data for developing theories of instruction. Such a record would also enable the supervising teacher to test out with students some of the emerging theories of instruction.

Expert knowledge of content in a discipline is widely acknowledged as a requisite for college teaching, but need for the college teacher to attain a high degree of expertness in the process of teaching has been voiced by a growing number of college and university administrators. With increasing interest in the improvement of the quality of instruction, the evidence from this study that much of the discourse was concerned with recall of factual data has implications for in-service education of the present faculty in nursing.

Exploring the Natural History Method as an Observational
and Analytical Tool for Teachers[1]

The aim of the study was to explore the potential of the natural history method as one means by which the classroom teacher might secure objective data about and analyze what is going on in his classroom. Selected subjects were trained to use participant observation and to analyze the data collected inductively. The training, as well as the results of the training, were described and analyzed to learn what questions should be asked of the method when used in this way.

The natural history method is an empirical, inductive approach to the study of social systems. It seeks to provide a complete, consistent description of a functioning system through gathering objective data, primarily via observation, in and about an on-going group, and analyzing

---

[1]The study had not been completed in its formal, written form at the time of this writing. For further information contact the author.

that data. What is to be observed is what goes on in a given environment: the events, their nature and order; the interaction, who says what or does what with or to whom, when, and where;[1] and the non-verbal and/or quasi-verbal communicators, e.g., gestures and intonations; all within the context of a time, a setting and a particular use of space. Within the method these aspects and their interrelationships are believed to give expression to the workings of the system and to provide the raw material from which analysis of the system, as it operates, may be made.

No pre-established categories or hypotheses guide the collection or analysis of the data. The observer looks for regularities and patterns of behavior, time, events, and use of space. Categories for ordering data, the variables of the system, and the hypotheses which explain the "rules" and processes of the system emerge from the data itself. As they do, substantive support for their existence is provided by the data. The resulting analysis provides a description of the system from within. The data and analyses are treated and presented as open records so that the data may be re-analyzed at any time.

Anthropologists and others for whom the natural history method is a tool of the discipline have detailed neither the program by which they were trained in the use of the method, nor the program which they use to train others. Consequently, a training program was devised for the conduct of the study.

---

[1]A partial restatement of a quotation by Robert H. Guest, "Categories of Events in Field Observation," Human Organization Research, Richard N. Adams and Jack J. Priess, eds. (Homewood, Illinois: The Dordey Press, 1960), p. 225.

Conduct of the Study

A group of twenty-seven students who selected the section of "Seminar in Education" taught by the author of the study became the population for the study. This seminar is a co-requisite of student teaching and together they terminate the pre-service teacher preparatory curricula at Eastern Michigan University. The seminar instructor was concurrently a college supervisor, but supervised only one of the twenty-seven students in the seminar.

The population involved ten men and seventeen women. They were student teaching in sixteen schools in ten school systems. Twelve were placed in senior high schools, two in kindergarten/pre-school situations, and one was jointly placed in a senior high school and an elementary school. Of the seventeen junior-senior high school placements, four were in social studies, three in physical education, three in business education, three in mathematics, two in English, one in science, and one in art. Nine of the twenty-seven subjects had taken their first course in the teacher preparatory sequence, educational psychology, with the instructor of the seminar.

The purpose and nature of the study and the activities that it would involve were presented to the potential subjects, on a general level, at the first class meeting. They agreed to participate in the project and the first step in the training program was initiated. The subjects were asked to select a class session from their student teaching experience when they would be teaching. They were directed to engage in observation and to prepare a report of that observation. They were asked to detail what occurred during that time as precisely as possible and to aim at objectively reporting what they did and said, to whom, when and where, and what their students did and said, to or with whom, when and where, in the order in which it occurred. No additional directions for accomplishing the task were provided as it seemed relevant to learn what abilities the subjects might exhibit in observing and reporting without special training, as a guide to determining the necessity for training and/or the nature of training required.

The observational reports were read and notations made on each indicating where the subject appeared to be successful in objectively reporting what occurred, where he seemed to have gaps in the narrative, was interpreting or summarizing rather than reporting fully and objectively, and how he might proceed in future observational activities. When the reports were returned to the subjects, the trainer spoke about the nature and value of objective observation. General praise was given to the subjects for the quantity and quality of their observations. Specific examples from the reports were recited, without identifying the particular reporter, and the subjects were asked to explain why these selections were pieces of objective observation, or interpretations, or the like. Their feelings about the activity and the problems they encountered in doing the activity were solicited, and suggestions were offered for eliminating the problems or modifying their impact. Supportive guidance was provided to allay doubts about ability to accomplish the task.

A film of a class-in-session was shown to the group. As with the previous activity, they were asked to observe as much of what occurred as they could. At the end of the film they were asked to relate, in detail and in order, what they had observed. Through pointed questions the

233

subjects were directed to compare their observations with those of the group, consider what they had missed and why they might have missed it, and note instances of interpretation and summarization rather than objective observation. They were directed to consider and verbalize a variety of observational details present in the film but overlooked in the verbal reports, e.g., use of space, use of time, physical environment. The intent of the activity was to provide a common, single experience for the group and through this to extend the dimensions of consideration in observation.

Arrangements were made to have the subjects view video-tapes of nine consecutive meetings of an elementary school group. Written directions were provided reiterating what they were to do and why they were doing it, and setting down some suggestions and directions for accomplishing the task. The tapes were intended to provide a common observational experience for the group and training experiences in observing and reporting an on-going situation. While this activity was underway, and throughout the study, the subjects freely initiated discussions about their problems and feelings in doing the activities. In attempting to deal with these both specific suggestions and supportive guidance were offered to the group and to individuals. When the completed observational reports of the video-taped sessions were examined, annotated and returned to the subjects, they were discussed, following the same procedures as those used with the first activity.

One session of the seminar provided an "unanticipated event" of relevance to the training. In the judgment of the instructor, the session had not been successful. At the following session, which was to be devoted to introducing the subjects to the analysis of observational data, this judgment was presented to the group and they were asked to "reconstruct" what had occurred during the preceding session and to evolve hypotheses, from the reconstruction, to explain how and why what had occurred had occurred. From this verbal exercise in observation and analysis, generalizations were made about the significance of objective observation and analysis, about the process of analysis, and about the relevance of the behavior of the teacher.

For the training session introducing analysis of data, the students were given observational data prepared by the instructor and asked to analyze the data. Written directions were provided for accomplishing the task. In presenting their analyses of the given data the subjects were required to provide evidence from the data to support their analyses about the patterns of behavior and interaction, and they were encouraged to compare and challenge each other's analyses. Questions about evolving hypotheses from data were explored and suggestions offered to aid the subjects in analyzing the observational reports they had collected through viewing the video-tapes, which constituted the next activity.

When the analyses of the on-going, video taped sessions were read, annotated, and returned to the subjects, they were discussed. Pointed questions based on examples culled from their analytic reports and verbal presentations were used to call attention to judgmental statements used in lieu of analyses, to the absence of supporting evidence, to conflicts in analyses among subjects, and to aspects which were overlooked.

All of the foregoing activities were intended to lead the subjects gradually and comfortably to the crux of the training program, participant observation and analysis of the data secured from participant observation. The subjects were directed to choose a class period from their student teaching situation to use for ten participant observational experiences, to engage in such observation, and to prepare an observational report of each session. At the completion of this activity they were to analyze the data secured. In preparation for these activities the process and mechanics of the method were reviewed, questions and problems discussed, and suggestions which might aid them offered.

The first self-observational report was read, annotated, and returned to the subjects as were the nine subsequent ones, before the analyses were required. Problems and limitations found in these reports were discussed with individuals and the group, and the process of analysis was again discussed with specific attention given to analyzing participant observational reports. When the analyses were completed, the seminar teacher read, annotated, and returned them to the subjects for their perusal. The last activity and the total project were discussed and critically evaluated by the subjects.

For the last session of seminar the subjects were asked to complete and return an anonymous evaluation form concerned with both the course and the project. Six months after the completion of the project the former subjects were asked to complete a questionnaire about the project in retrospect.

Analysis of the Data

The nature and construct of the study suggested an inductive approach to its analysis; one which would approach the data as in the

natural history method. Given an exploratory study, a limited population, an unvalidated training program and an informal design, it was
imperative that the data collected in the course of the study yield as
many questions and dimensions to consider as it could. It was decided
to begin to analyze the data in at least three stages: (1) tabulate the
information secured, set down and hopefully transcend "first impressions,"
and raise questions arising from these processes; (2) analyze the data
formally and evolve questions to be asked of it; (3) seek answers, from
the data, to the questions raised. And, it was considered wise to allow
the steps and stages of analysis to suggest further steps and stages.

Data available for analysis included: (1) six written activities
produced by the subjects (a pre-training participant observational report,
observational reports of nine video-taped sessions of an on-going group,
and analysis of observational data given to the subject, ten participant
observation reports, and analysis of participant observation); (2) information about the subjects (forms concerning their background, preparation,
and experiences with children and youth, assembled by the University as
their "Student Teaching Folder," and a "Personal Information Form" they
completed at the inception of the study); (3) impressions of the project
in its concept and conduct (an anonymous "Evaluation Form" completed at
the end of the study and a "Questionnaire" completed six months later);
and (4) a "Plan Book/Diary" maintained by the trainer.

The majority of the data was collected, but there were omissions
in particular areas. Twenty subjects completed all of the six activities,
three completed five, three completed four and one completed but two. One
of the twenty-seven "Student Teaching Folders" had been lost by the

University, but all of the "Personal Information Forms" were secured. Twenty-three subjects completed the anonymous "Evaluation Form," but only seventeen returned the "Questionnaire." The trainer's "Plan Book/Diary" was secured.

At the first stage in the analysis all of the data collected, except for the "Questionnaire," were perused, with notes and reactions recorded. Information about each of the subjects was tabulated, e.g., sex, age, nature of preparation, student teaching placement, and a number arbitrarily assigned to him for use in the tables constructed and in the second stage of analysis. Responses and comments to the questions asked in the anonymous "Evaluation Form" were tallied. Throughout, questions which arose from this first, informal reading of the data were noted and filed separately. The data were then put away for a period of time.

For the second stage, to derive some assessment of the results of the training program, a method for evaluating the six written activities produced by the subjects was devised. Each of the activities was evaluated and compared with like activities for each subject. The results of training were then assessed for the group. The individual and group assessments were compared with the factual data tabulated in the first stage of a search for patterns and questions to ask.

The answers and comments to each question of the "Questionnaire" were tabulated and analyzed, for the group and for each project. The relationship among answers in individual "Questionnaires" and for the group were examined and compared with an analysis of the questions. The relationships between answers and possible patterns of sex, those who were and were not teaching, and those who had or had not been former students were explored. The results of these analyses were compared with the results of the analysis of the six written assignments.

The answers and comments to the questions asked in the anonymous "Evaluation Form" were analyzed by question and the answers within each form were compared. The patterns of answers were compared to an analysis of the questions and to answers given to another portion of the form concerned with the subject's impressions of the course as a whole. The results were compared with the analyses of the "Questionnaire" for the group, to learn if changes in impression had taken place with the passage of time and change in status.

In analyzing the trainer's "Plan Book/Diary," categories relative to the content of the training program, subject reactions, and impressions of aspects of the project were suggested; the trainer's reactions to and impressions of the project as a whole and in its parts were noted. The three categories were then compared and interrelated. The resultant analysis was compared with the analyses of the "Evaluation Form" and data from the "Questionnaire."

At each step within the second stage of analysis questions arising from the data were noted. For the third stage all questions that had been raised and noted in prior stages guided a re-examination of the data amassed. Since the second and third stages continue to generate dimensions of analysis to be undertaken, the analysis, and consequently this description, is incomplete at this time.

Findings: To Date

If the generating of questions about the potential use of one natural history method as a tool for observing and analyzing what occurs in the classroom is a primary aim of the study, the study might be said to be enormously, even overwhelmingly successful at this point. The number and diversity of questions suggested by the data are a source of delight and frustration.

In assessing the results of training prospective teachers to observe and analyze by study of their written activities, a highly varied picture emerges. While one subject was a fairly good observer prior to training and continued to expand his abilities during training, the remainder of the subjects were poor observers prior to training. A majority of them improved their observational skills, but the amount and kind of improvement varied greatly from one subject to the next. A sizeable minority made no improvement in their ability to observe objectively, and several seemed to improve and then to decline in ability during the course of the activities. In terms of what was observed, while there was a general extension in details and dimensions, there was a tendency to focus either on the teacher or on the students, and the focus did not necessarily remain constant throughout the observational activities. This situation was replicated in the analytical activities, but was further complicated by the fact that there was little consistency between observational and analytical patterns of performance. Subjects who improved in observation did not necessarily improve in analysis, and some who did not improve in observation seemed to exhibit increased skill in analysis. In general, there was less improvement in ability to analyze than in ability to observe objectively. In the analyses of participant observation, there was a decided tendency to avoid analyzing the teacher's, i.e., their own, behavior.

What factors might account for the results of training obtained? How is it one student was a good observer, without previous training, and some students were skilled analyzers and poor observers? What might account for the range exhibited in progress or lack of progress? Differences in ability to observe and analyze did not appear to reflect the sex, teaching level, subject matter preparation, or former experience of a subject with the trainer. Might there be personality factors which open or limit a trainee's receptivity to and readiness for observation and analysis of his own behavior?

The unwillingness or inability of some of the subjects to analyze their own behavior as teachers, leads one to question why. It may be that the activity presents too great a "threat," particularly in a "new" teacher. Perhaps the subjects had not learned to see examination of the teacher's behavior as a significant, manipulable factor in teaching.

The subjects' appraisals of their training in participant observation provide more consistent results and suggest that there was no necessary relationship between their performance and the value they perceived in the training. As expressed in the anonymous "Evaluation Form," twenty of the twenty-three respondents felt that they had learned from involvement in the training, had found it to be of interest, saw participant observation and analysis as relevant and practical to the teacher, and had found the skills to be of help in their student teaching. With regard to the time required to learn the skills and to prepare the activities, the

241

subjects reported that the activities were too time-consuming and they
questioned whether the time required justified the value of the activities,
particularly the video-tapes. Their responses six months later suggested
that the strong, positive impressions of the training had remained and
negative feelings about the amount of time required had lessened. Seventy-
six percent of the respondents were officially teaching six months after
their training, and 94 percent of these indicated that they had already
found the skills to be of value to them personally or in their teaching.
Most respondents listed more than one use they had found for the skills,
primarily in their work as teachers, and all of the uses were related to
the method as taught.

What factors might account for the striking difference between the
subjects' performance and their impressions of the project? Were the
subjects able to see the value of the skills and method, though not yet
able to perform in line with their understanding and acceptance? This
appears to be so and may be a factor in the disparities indicated in performance. Still, one questions whether other factors may also be operat-
ing. Two questions might be raised: To what extent may the subjects'
impressions reflect their notions of "playing the student game" appropriately? What influence might the trainer's personality and manner have on
the students' impressions? And, what if the two questions are linked?

Foreshadowing these questions are questions raised about the training program and the conduct of the study, by the results of training, the
subjects' impressions and the trainer's "Plan Book/Diary." At this point
one must seriously question the nature and quality of the training program
devised and whether the program was too ambitious for the time available.

Did the pacing of activities fail to provide enough time for each of the skills to be developed properly? How well were the skills taught? Were the activities used to train the subjects the best choices, ones which took advantage of situations that would seem most relevant to the subjects and help them to see the potential of the method or the skills as they might be used by the teacher? One suspects that to be successful the training method must extend over a longer period of time, with considerably more practice provided in using the method as it is to be used.

Implications of the Two Studies

At the beginning of the chapter certain questions were posed: Who is to guide the novice in the study of teaching? What role(s) is he to play? What responsibilities does he have? How is he to proceed in the various settings in which teaching is to be studied. The courses and programs directed to the study of teaching examined earlier in the chapter yielded some inferences about the answers to these questions. The view of the work of the college supervisor as teacher, and the changes that are occurring in such classes, suggested parallels between the college supervisor as teacher and the inferred teacher of classes directed to the study of teaching. The two studies presented lent support to the inferences and parallels suggested and expanded the potential answers to these questions.

If the study of teaching becomes or is to become a focus of teacher education, ideally all who are involved in the education and preparation of teachers should bear responsibility for guiding the novice in the study of teaching. The Hill study suggests that the teacher of teachers sets the model for the level of thinking. The Mertz study suggests that to learn the skills needed to study teaching using one or a complex of systems to secure and analyze objective data about what is going on in one's classroom requires a carefully constructed training program and supervised practice over a period of time. It seems apparent that one training course or experience in which the approach is presented and used, or one model of a teacher that the prospective teacher is to become, is totally insufficient. Certainly, all of the teachers involved in the professional sequence are influential models and all should be able to make systematic observation and analysis of teaching behavior. The college supervisor is singularly important. His work with students in their laboratory experiences requires him to provide them with objective feedback about their practice and he may provide such feedback by use of selected systems and techniques in his visits and conferences. He has the ties to the university that are necessary to influence programs. He has the intimate knowledge of teaching practice generally, and the teaching as practiced by the particular students that enable him to recommend and evaluate as well as teach the techniques, models, or systems which emerge.

The various methods developed are intended to provide the prospective teacher with the processes and tools needed for becoming and remaining a student of teaching, a clinical researcher in-service. The systems involve skills to be learned and practiced. If the teacher is to maintain the level of skill use attained during pre-service preparation, he must be encouraged in his in-service situation to continue to use the skills; and he would profit from periodic supervision of their use. As systems become more sophisticated and more is learned about how teaching may best be studied, teachers in-service will require opportunities to learn new techniques, skills, and devices for improving their ability to study their practice of teaching. The college supervisor's association with schools provides both the entry to and continuity with former students that may prove invaluable in continuing or renewing training.

A single technique, system, or model for analyzing teaching may prove inadequate or unsuitable as an approach to preparing teachers to become students of teaching. It may be that a complex of systems, selected to meet a particular teaching situation and teacher will provide the best means of studying teaching. With an individualized approach the teacher of classes directed to the study of teaching will not only have to be prepared to teach a variety of systems, but will have to be able to assist the prospective teacher in selecting the systems appropriate for him. Probably more important will be the ability to guide prospective teachers in developing their own approaches to study of their teaching behavior.

The role of trainer alters and redefines the role of evaluator traditionally played by the teacher of teachers. Emerging schemes require that judgments be made in terms of pre-established criteria, with the results of analysis of practice used to determine whether or not the criteria have been met. The burden of evaluation falls on the shoulders of the "researcher," i.e., the student, rather than the trainer, while the trainer serves as guide or assistant to the student in determining criteria and in assessing their fulfillment. This shift in responsibility may require the teacher of teachers to assume a role long played by the college supervisor, "supportive therapist." When a teacher looks at his own behavior and is no longer able to blame the resulting evaluation on an

245

"outsider," the levels of threat and feelings of insecurity or inadequacy may become significant. While it is quite probable that one analyzes only to the point of what one can accept, with continued use and guidance, new dimensions may be seen. The student of teaching may need someone to help him to keep the results of his analyses in perspective and at levels of threat that will not incapacitate him. And, particularly at times of widening self-analysis, the teacher may require assistance in devising strategies to alter patterns and choose methods to replace those he found inappropriate as a result of his analyses.

The teacher of classes and seminars devoted to the study of teaching must be a model of the teacher he wishes the student to become. He must study teaching as he practices it in his classes and seminars. The student needs to see the relevance of such study to the practice of teaching. There is much to suggest that the class directed to the study of teaching be conducted as a cooperative study of teaching by the teacher and the students.

The college supervisor who is teaching classes is in a crucial position now, relative to the study of teaching. He is already using systems of observation and analysis in his supervisory role and he has the ties with the university, schools, and students in-the-field that are required. He is in a near-perfect in-between position. Whether or not he will move his classes, and other classes in the preparatory curricula, in the direction of the study of teaching will depend on a host of factors, both within and outside of his control, but he will nonetheless be in a position to have an enormous impact upon such a determination.

Chapter VIII

REFLECTIONS

Margaret Lindsey

Reflection on the studies reported in this monograph is both sobering and rewarding. Thinking about them results in disconcerting feelings,
even some discouragement. Yet, individually and collectively, they fur-
nish a stimulus to continued and intensified effort. They portray a
struggle to break open for inspection one dimension of a critical component
of professional teacher education, laboratory experiences. Because that
component is so important, further examination of what has been reported
here should be useful. Consideration of ways to build on the basic
knowledge derived from these studies should prove beneficial to students
of the field.

Reflections on the Procedures and
Findings of the Studies

The difficulties encountered in developing appropriate means for
studying behavior in the professional laboratory would be cause enough for
turning one's back on the problem were it not for the conviction that it
can and must be done. The road between what we know and what we need to
know about teaching and learning in teacher education laboratories is long

and tortuous. But, scholarship demands that it be traveled. What have
been viewed as impasses must now be confronted and mastered.

Of the difficulties that have plagued investigators few are more
persistent or baffling than the presence of many hard-to-control variables
in a situation where human beings are interacting. Coupled with the
diversity existing even when situations are expected to be "like,"
"similar," or "comparable," the hazard of multiple, seemingly intangible
variables has been a primary cause for avoiding study of relationships
between student and teacher performance in the laboratory. Although a
setting is narrowly confined, the human beings limited to two, and the
focus of their encounter strictly defined, the variables often present the
researcher with an almost impossible range of potentially relevant data.
Once detailed study is made of the two persons interacting in a reasonably
controlled situation, there is the question of how representative their
interaction is. Would either the processes of their interaction or the
substance of it be found in similar situations? If so, would the relationships between one set of variables and another remain constant from an
experimental setting to other settings?

Reflection on this particular persistent problem ought to be couched
in a framework of anticipated outcomes. That is to say, how one views the
difficulty and the decisions he makes as he undertakes systematic study
are a product of what he is seeking to do. If the intent is to produce
significant knowledge that has high level, valid generalizability, stipula-
tions as to the character of the research are built into the intent. If,
on the other hand, an investigator limits his research to examination of
his own practice for the purpose of improving that practice, his research

248

may be quite different in character. It may meet all the scholar's
standards of rigor but his findings will be unique to him and his setting
rather than generalizable to others rather like him in other similar
settings. Sometimes the intent of a researcher is to demonstrate
methodology or to develop instruments, rather than to produce findings in
the form of verified knowledge. When this is the case, the researcher
expects that what he has demonstrated by way of method and/or what he has
developed by way of valid and reliable instruments might be employed by
others who wish to investigate the same or similar problems. These three
different anticipated outcomes of research are not inclusive, for there
are others. Neither are they unrelated, because methodologies and findings
in one kind of study may use, as well as contribute to, other types of
study. Nor is a hierarchy implied; each intent has merit in its own right.

Clearly the studies reported in the previous five chapters were not
designed with the first intent in mind, that is, to produce valid
generalizable findings. Rather, the dominant purpose was to demonstrate a
set of procedures that might be used by anyone wishing to examine the
verbal behavior of supervisors and students in a teacher education laboratory. Instruments developed in the several studies are responsive to the
particularities of the situations in which they were developed. This
being the case, other investigators may choose to use them, or they may
elect not to use them, favoring only replication of the procedures in
developing their own models or systems of categories. It may well be,
indeed it is hoped, that further research using some of the means described
in this monograph will produce instruments of sufficient validity to enable
their use in many situations.

249

As has been reiterated throughout this monograph, supervision in a teacher education laboratory is viewed as teaching teachers about teaching, and as such, it can and should be subjected to systematic inquiry. If even a limited number of supervisors accept this point of view and take it seriously enough to initiate study of their own behavior by use of procedures suggested in these studies or other procedures, these studies will have made an important contribution. If the instruments developed here are subjected to rigorous testing in various settings, and a process of repeated revisions brings them, or any one of them to a level of validity that warrants general use, this will be an additional contribution.

A second kind of persistent problem for those who would inquire into interaction among human beings and the possible consequences of that interaction is the avowed cruciality of the climate, atmosphere, feelings, personal congruence or lack of it, and other such factors. Few would question the importance of interpersonal relationships, the view each participant has of himself and his competence, the respect or lack of respect each has for the other, the presence or absence of warmth and affection, and the unspoken encouragement and support. But these conditions must be inferred from behavior or reliance must be placed on self-reports. Behavior that contributes to an atmosphere of mutual regard is elusive; making valid inferences calls for atypically skilled persons; and self-reports have limitations.

Given the difficulty of identifying the affective dimensions of a social encounter, and the more troublesome task of describing them with objectivity and accuracy, investigators have generally turned their attention to those matters that are more susceptible to close examination. In all probability this accounts in no small degree for the vast amount of research on teaching that is limited to analysis of tapescripts of classroom verbal behavior.

This is exactly what was done by the investigators who have reported their studies in the preceding chapters. It was recognized by all that the personal relationships and climate were of utmost importance in setting the stage for and in determining what happened in supervisory teaching situations. Also recognized was the fact that verbal behavior has affective dimensions and can be analyzed for what it implies. Still it was decided to avoid trying to deal either directly or indirectly with personal, affective aspects of the teaching by supervisors. Instead, focus was deliberately placed on the language of the interaction and further limited to what was explicit in that language. Doubtless such a focus is important but the results must be interpreted within the limits of the focus.

Often during the process of analyzing the linguistic discourse of supervisory conferences investigators commented, "So much depends on how it was said." Comments like these were repeated frequently: "You really have to know the student." "You need to know why the supervisor said what he did." "This can't be classified without knowing what went on before." At one point, it was said, "I know for a fact that this supervisor has warm and wonderful relations with this student teacher, yet from this protocol you get an opposite impression."

Audiotape recordings were used as data in these studies. Recordings on videotape would provide considerable additional data. Even with complete audio-visual recordings, however, much that is essential to interpretation of what is going on at the moment is not recorded: for example, the relationships that have been built over time between supervisor and student or between teacher and pupils in a classroom; the depth of understanding of an individual's needs that underlies a given teaching behavior; or the remote factors in a university or in a school that influence behavior.

The many unknowns confronted by the researcher when analyzing teaching behavior provide no reason for abandoning the effort to learn what can be learned from such analysis. There is reason for caution in stating findings and interpreting their meanings for practice. There is reason also for increasing attention to other than verbal behavior, so that more comprehensive interpretations of findings and their implications for teaching behavior may be possible.

A characteristic of much of the reported research on teaching behavior, and of these studies as well, is the quantification of findings. Obviously quantification provides information. In the present studies, for example, the data reveal what proportion of time the supervisors being studied spent talking with their students about specified topics, how often supervisory language was prescriptive as compared with descriptive, and so on. It is useful for supervisors to examine quantitative data about their own behavior and to bring to the examination questions that cause them to be self-critical.

Important as quantified findings are for many purposes, they are intended in most studies of teaching (as they are in these studies) to be no more than descriptive. In and of themselves they do not have a value orientation. It is the interpreter-consumer who brings his values to the examination of quantified descriptive findings, and in so doing he is obliged to recognize that he is applying his values to data that are intended to be value-free. The intention to deal with descriptive data without a value orientation is not always realized, of course. Nevertheless, in these studies, as in other similar ones, the need for caution in attaching values to quantified descriptive data should be underscored.

Among the many difficulties investigators face in attempts to describe behavior of supervisory teaching and to establish valid relationships among variables in complex situations, only three have been commented upon here. In the studies reported in this monograph, these difficulties were present, and they were treated with varying degrees of success, or not at all. This does not diminish the value of the studies; it rather supports the urgency of continued effort to deal in effective ways with the problems identified.

Potential Contributions of the Procedures and Findings of the Studies

In Chapter I, it was argued that professional laboratories of all kinds and students' experience in them would be taking on more, not less, importance in the years immediately ahead. The critical importance of the guidance students have available in planning for and examining their laboratory experiences was emphasized. This latter point was elaborated in Chapter II, where a position was taken that the central function of designated personnel (supervisors) in the professional laboratory is teaching teachers about teaching. The five intervening chapters report studies designed to demonstrate selected ways in which supervisors might examine their behavior as they teach prospective teachers about teaching. A question worthy of some reflection is: What specific contributions might these studies, and others similar to them, make to the improvement of the guidance supervisors provide students in a laboratory?

Discussion in the preceding section of this chapter has supplied a few hints on some possible answers to the question. For example, it has been suggested that supervisors might study their own teaching behavior by means of procedures developed in these studies. The least effect of such study would surely be a new awareness by the supervisor of his behavior, and sensitivity to his behavior is a prerequisite to his taking steps to improve it. A few illustrations of the kinds of inquiry supervisors might conduct by systematic study of their teaching behavior follow.

It is often said that one sees what he is able to see, or that he sees what he wants to see. What persons see as they observe in classrooms or other laboratory settings is witness to the truth of those statements. While any two individuals observing in the same situation may see some things in common, the likelihood is great that there also will be differences in what they see. If supervisors and students are to examine what has gone on in the laboratory, it is desirable that they have adequate data for checking their perceptions. The more their perceptions of the situation can be brought into agreement, the greater the chance that their language in discourse has common referents. Using concrete, objectively recorded data as the substance of discussion helps in clarifying perceptions. A supervisor's analysis of his interaction with a student may cause him to discover that a problem of variation in perception was present. Such discovery, it may be assumed, will make a supervisor more alert to the need for checking perceptions, his own and others', before he proceeds too far with his teaching.

254

Students sometimes indicate there is little value in talking with their supervisors. Any number of reasons may account for this feeling on their part. For example, it may be that almost no help is provided, that the same things are discussed over and over, that comments are so general as to be almost meaningless, that one time after another prescriptions of what is to be done are handed out without any rationale, that the things selected for discussion are not seen as important or interesting, that the supervisor does all the talking and seldom listens, or that he uses the time to air his own problems. Any sensitive supervisor will be aware of such feelings on the part of students he works with, and of course will try to understand their causes. Although causation may lie elsewhere, a supervisor is responsible for examination of his own behavior as a possible source of difficulty contributing to the student's feelings about the worthlessness of conversation with him. If he will record his own teaching, just as he asks his students to record their behavior, and if he will subject records to analysis, the chances are he will learn quite a bit about causes of student feeling.

Today in teacher education programs much emphasis is placed on cognitive processes. Particularly students-in-training are having exposure to such ideas, for example, as "the way a teacher asks a question sets the expectancy for the cognitive process pupils will use in responding." Students are expected to build skill in asking questions that will elicit from pupils a range of cognitive processes, and especially to cause pupils to lift levels of thinking. This being the case, it is reasonable to expect that supervisors practice such skill in their dialogue with students. But do they? The same question can be asked about many other kinds of behavior which students are taught to believe are desirable in teaching. Do their supervisors demonstrate these behaviors? The serious supervisor will ask himself such questions and he will go on to seek answers by systematic study of his supervisory teaching behavior. If he is really on a team basis with his student, he will have him share in the analysis. What better way could he drive home the idea that one can learn from study of his behavior?

Over a considerable period of time, information has been gathered on what both supervisors and their students view as problems when they undertake work in a laboratory with pupils. There has been general agreement on these problems: lesson planning, discipline (control, management), and methods. What often happens is that the preactive task of planning for teaching takes on disproportionate importance in the encounters between students and those who work with them. Also, discipline frequently becomes a topic on which there is general advice to do certain things and not to do others, or it is discussed purely on the basis of the superficial manifestations of a problem. When pupil-teacher interaction in the laboratory is discussed, it too often is a matter of dealing with a supervisor's general impressions from exceedingly limited observational data. What do supervisors focus on as the substance of their teaching? Do they make sure that over a period of time they and their students have worked on more than generalities, have dealt in depth with important teaching behaviors, have given direct attention to the art of teaching? Any supervisor who has the initiative and ambition can obtain reliable answers to such questions. And, if he is a student of his own practice, he will.

Completely different problems evolve from the organization of student teaching programs, the placing of students in widely scattered schools as laboratories, and the assignment to both school and college personnel of responsibility for their guidance. Within current patterns, typically a student teacher works closely with at least two persons: a classroom teacher and a college supervisor. What are the particular functions to be performed by these two supervisors? If they operate as a team, as of course they should, the assumption is that each brings to the work with the student a special kind of contribution and that the specialties are complementary and supporting; certainly not in disharmony or negating. What too often happens in practice is that the two supervisors work independently with the student, neither informed as to what the other is doing. Commonly the result is unnecessary duplication of effort; sometimes one unconsciously tears down what the other has done.

At a time when competent personnel are not in oversupply and financing professional education programs is difficult, it would seem inexcusable to allow the conditions just mentioned to exist. What is it that college personnel can and should do with students who are in professional laboratories? What unique contributions can they make? What roles should classroom teachers supervising students be expected to assume? Are both these persons essential in their present roles? What in fact do they do? As in dealing with most problems, here, too, it is required that evidence be available on what the facts are and that suggestions for dealing with the situation take adequate account of the facts. Teams of supervisors, together with their students or alone, might examine what overlapping exists in their work, might search for understandings about the unique contributions of persons in different positions, and might gain insight into the need for more and better channels of communication. These things supervisors can do by use of procedures suggested in these studies.

The foregoing kinds of inquiry supervisors might make by application of ideas, methods, and/or instruments developed in the studies reported in this monograph are illustrative. The sum of the illustrations, and others that might have been given, suggests that supervisors, as teachers, need to be scholarly about their own practice as well as to try to help their students be scholarly about their practice. Procedures used in the reported studies are narrowly focused, but a supervisor need not confine his examination of his behavior to verbal exchange in conferring with students. He is free to extend his own inquiry to those problems of concern to him and to develop his own methods for collecting and analyzing data on his own behavior. In the expectation that this will occur lies hope for impressive gains in individualized teaching of future teachers.

PROJECTION

The stream of research of which these studies were a part continues. Further exploratory studies designed to learn as much as possible in given situations about relationships between supervisory and student behaviors are in progress. Other activities are geared to validation of instruments with the expectancy that eventually they may be more widely applicable to supervisory behavior. Experimentation is going on in several centers to discover the value or lack of value in using the study procedures and instruments in the training of supervisors.

In the series of monographs, <u>Supervision in Teacher Education Laboratories</u>, the second publication reports a completely theoretical analysis. Its author, Gilles Dussault, brings together in a most useful pattern, and for the first time, what is known (findings from research) and what is asserted (professional opinion) about supervisor's work with student teachers. In an effort to provide direction for future research, he turns to Carl Rogers' theory of therapy and personality change. From that model theory he develops a middle-range theory of supervision in teacher education. His final chapter makes specific proposals on what studies are needed and how these studies should be carried out if the unknowns are to become knowns.

The anticipated date of publication for the third monograph in the series is October 1970. Based on the studies and the theoretical model developed by Dussault, that monograph will propose a program for the specialized preparation of supervisors for work in teacher education laboratories.

Appendix

SYSTEMS OF CATEGORIES FOR THE DESCRIPTION AND
ANALYSIS OF SUPERVISORY TEACHING IN
TEACHER EDUCATION LABORATORIES

PRINCIPLES OF LEARNING AS THE BASIS FOR ANALYSIS OF TEACHING
BEHAVIOR IN TUTORIAL SESSIONS WITH STUDENT TEACHERS

James K. Canfield
Arlene F. Low
Robert E. Mullin

Selected Principles

1. Learning is facilitated when the learner responds actively in the learning situation.

2. A learner's chances of learning are increased when his purposes and those of the teacher are sufficiently similar for him to perceive the relationship.

3. A learner's chances of learning are increased when the material to be learned is meaningful to him.

4. A learner's chances of learning are increased when he can see some possibility of succeeding in the learning task he is attempting.

5. A learner's chances of learning are increased each time he experiences success in a learning task.

6. A learner's chances of learning are increased when he has opportunities for and assistance in the discovery of facts, relationships, and generalizations.

7. Possibility of the retention of learned material is increased when the learner practices his learning immediately, frequently, and in varied situations.

Definition:

Principles of learning, as used in this study, are generalizations, based on research findings, and generally accepted by learning theorists, which state positive relationships between certain environmental conditions which can be manipulated by the teacher, and the acquisition, retention and/or transfer, by learners in school situations, of facts, concepts, or generalizations.

Key for Analysis:

      / The teacher manipulated the environmental conditions, so
        as to facilitate positive relationships between variables
        implied by the principle.

      - The teacher failed to manipulate the conditions so as to
        facilitate positive relationships between variables implied
        by the principle.

      0 The teacher was non-sensitive to the opportunity to manipulate
        the conditions so as to facilitate positive relationships
        between variables implied by the principle.

TEACHER MOVES AND COGNITIVE PROCESSES OF PUPILS AS
BASES FOR ANALYSIS OF TEACHING BEHAVIOR IN
TUTORIAL SESSIONS WITH STUDENT TEACHERS

Anna Beth Brown
Margaret Cobban
Floyd Waterman

Pedagogical Moves[1]

Structuring--serves the pedagogical function of setting the context
        for subsequent behavior.

Soliciting --elicits a response.

Responding --bears a reciprocal relationship to soliciting moves and
        occurs only in relation to them.

Reacting   --occasioned by a structuring, soliciting, responding, or
        prior reacting move; serves to modify and/or to rate what
        has been said previously.

Cognitive Processes of Pupils

1. Perceiving, recalling, recognizing. The speaker selects
     certain stimuli from his environment through the use of

----

[1] Arno A. Bellack et al., The Language of the Classroom (New York:
Teachers College Press, Teachers College, Columbia University, 1966).

his senses and brings them to the conscious level by verbal
description. He calls back to memory by recollecting observations from previous experience. He is aware that the conditions observed are the same as those previously known.

2. <u>Discriminating, comparing, defining</u>. The speaker selects
   distinguishing features from the more general features of
   ideas or phenomena; he examines for similarities; he names,
   describes, or states his perception of the general and specific
   features of ideas or phenomena.

3. <u>Classifying, relating, generalizing</u>. The speaker puts
   together groups of ideas, events, and situations that
   have characteristics in common. He shows the connection
   between one situation and another and views the situation
   as a whole by combining ideas, events, and elements into a
   unified statement.

4. <u>Opining, judging, evaluating</u>. The speaker holds a conclusion
   with confidence but it is not always based upon extensive
   evidence. He deliberates and asserts his decision on the
   basis of some criteria; he appraises carefully and makes
   quantitative decisions upon criteria.

5. <u>Inferring, interpreting, applying</u>. The speaker surmises
   probable consequences through reasoning. He translates
   previous experience or ideas into new forms, and he employs
   for a particular purpose a previous idea, or he makes a
   connection by bringing to bear previous experience.

A MODEL FOR ANALYZING AND DESCRIBING VERBAL INTERACTION BETWEEN COLLEGE SUPERVISORS AND STUDENT TEACHERS

Richard Verne Brown
Miriam Schaad Hoffman

Problem Solving Domain

Comprehending Processes

Identifying Procedures--participants verbalize problems for discussion. Such statements or restatements merely indicate an awareness of existing problems.

Defining Procedures--supervisors or students attempt to clarify problems through data gathering techniques such as searching, investigating, questioning, advising, suggesting, and information giving.

Analyzing Processes

Interpreting Procedures--participants attempt to gain insights into problems by diagnosing and assessing performance in terms of stated objectives.

Hypothesizing Procedures--supervisors or teachers try to postulate action hypotheses based upon identified existing relationships among various factors.

Affective Domain

Catharsis Procedures--endeavors of either participant to verbalize his emotions, motivations, feelings, and thoughts related to problems under discussion.

Rapport Building Procedures--supportive statements by college supervisors which afford confidence and security for teachers.

Social Amenities Procedures--polite formalities such as friendly conversations, greetings, and socializing.

Structuring Domain

Routine Processes

Administrative Procedures—focus on the development of policy
concerning role expectations; establish standards; scheduling;
attending to physical arrangements.

Summary Procedures—recapitulation of major points made during
problem solving.

Directing Processes

Leading Procedures—attempts by either participant to persuade
or encourage the other to choose topics for discussion and reach
decisions concerning the solution of chosen topics.

Controlling Procedures—attempts to direct teacher behavior
in a forceful manner through regulatory statements such as
applying sanctions, reprimanding, and taking corrective action.

A SYSTEM OF CATEGORIES FOR ANALYZING AND DESCRIBING THE
TEACHING BEHAVIOR OF COOPERATING TEACHERS
WITH STUDENT TEACHERS

Ruth Ann Heidelbach

Operational Verbal Behavior

The three functions of Operational Verbal Behavior are FOCUSING, DESCRIB-
ING, and PRESCRIBING.

FOCUSING OPERATIONS—call attention to the substantive area to be discussed.

Referring—to denote, allude to, or initiate talk about a
definition, an explanation, an inference, a logical
relationship, a summary, a proposal or hypothesis, a
generalization, an evaluation, a reaction, an agreement
or disagreement, or a restatement.

Asking—to inquire, examine, solicit, invite or investigate
a definition, an explanation, an inference, a logical
relationship, a summary, a proposal or hypothesis, a
generalization, an evaluation, a reaction, an agreement
or disagreement, or a restatement.

DESCRIBING OPERATIONS--order the phenomena of the substantive talk.

Clarifying--to interpret, explain, reason, infer, or imply.

Defining--to describe, portray, or identify.

Summarizing--to recapitulate, draw together ideas that have been discussed.

Agreeing.
Disagreeing.

Restating--to say again something that has been said earlier; repeating the verbal behavior of cooperating teacher or student.

Reacting--to indicate approval, disapproval, feeling about something that has been said or done.

PRESCRIBING OPERATIONS--indicate suggested or appropriate teaching behavior for the student teacher, the cooperating teacher, or teachers in general.

To think or guess that a teaching behavior should take place.

To consider a proposal for teaching behavior.

To make a definite proposal for behavior of student teacher, cooperating teacher, or other teachers.

To anticipate, conjecture, hypothesize, based on evidence, an appropriate teaching behavior.

To generalize and propose specific teaching behavior.

Substantive Areas

Substantive Areas indicate what the participants are talking, or have talked, about.

TEACHING BEHAVIORS

Interactive Teaching Behaviors--teaching that takes place in individualized, small group, or class situations.

Student teacher's teaching behavior.
Supervisor's teaching behavior.
Cooperating teacher's teaching behavior.
Generalizations about teaching behavior.
Team teaching.

<u>Schematic Teaching Behavior</u>--planning lessons or units of work; establishing routines; assessing and evaluating; any teaching behavior that is <u>not</u> interactive.

> Student teacher.
> Supervisor.
> Cooperating teacher.
> Other teachers.
> Team teaching.

BACKGROUND AND CHARACTERISTICS OF PUPILS AND/OR STUDENT TEACHER--talk that relates to background and characteristics of learners at any level and in any situation.

> Cognitive structure.
> Social structure.
> Psychological structure.
> Physical structure.

CURRICULUM CONTENT--talk about the curriculum of the elementary school or of the college.

> Knowledge.
> Skills.
> Attitudes.

ORGANIZATION AND ADMINISTRATION OF INSTRUCTION--the organization and administration of the elementary school and the college program from which the student teachers come.

> Instructional: Modes.
> Lessons.
> Units.
> Curricular designs.

> Administrative: Interactive.
> Schematic.

INSTRUCTIONAL MATERIALS--talk about materials of instruction for pupils or for students

> Use of media and materials.
> Production of media and materials.

A MODEL FOR ANALYZING AND DESCRIBING THE LINGUISTIC DISCOURSE
BETWEEN COLLEGE SUPERVISORS AND COOPERATING TEACHERS

Theodora Randall Kimsey

Interactive Dimension

State--give information.

Complete--summarize; add to an informational statement.

Question--seek information.

React--show agreement (or disagreement) with or approval (or disapproval)
of information given.

Logical Dimension

Report--to describe, generalize, and/or interpret (give an inference,
conjecture, hypothesis, and/or explanation with regard to) an
event, action, person, or state of affairs in the present or
in the past.

Evaluate--to rate or grade (use value words or comparative form of
sentence structure to describe) an event, action, person, or
state of affairs in the present or in the past.

Prescribe--to suggest what could or should have been with regard to an
event, action, person, or state of affairs in the present or in
the past.

Plan--to suggest what can, might, or will be in the future.

Substantive Dimension

Supervising Behavior--general and specific information about the roles
and responsibilities of supervisors (nature of supervisory behavior;
reasons for, purposes of, and effects of supervisory behavior;
feelings or concerns of supervisors about their work with students).

1. Cooperating Teacher Supervising Behavior

    a. General--general comments about the work of the participat-
       ing teacher.

b. Student--information about the participating teacher's work with the student currently assigned to him.

c. Concerns--general or specific information about the participating cooperating teacher's concerns about her work as a supervisor.

d. Observation/Conference--information about the behavior of the cooperating teacher during observation of the student or during conferences with the supervisor.

2. College Supervisor Supervising Behavior

a. General--general comments about the work and behavior of the participating college supervisor.

b. Student--general and specific information about the communications between the college supervisor and the student assigned to the participating teacher.

c. Concerns--general and specific information about the college supervisor's concerns with regard to his work as a college supervisor.

d. Observation/Conference--information about the behavior of the college supervisor during observation of the student or during conference with the cooperating teacher.

3. Cooperating Teacher-College Supervisor Team Behavior--information about the teamwork of the cooperating teacher and college supervisor in working with student(s) in the cooperating teacher's classroom.

Teaching Behavior--general and specific information about the teacher role, such as the nature of teaching behavior, reasons for, purposes of, effects of teaching behavior, and feelings and concerns of teachers about their work with pupils.

1. Student Teacher Teaching Behavior

a. General--general comments about the work or behavior of the student teacher.

b. Planning--information about the planning and preparation done by the student for work with pupils.

c. Content--concepts and behaviors this student teacher taught or will teach in a special curriculum area.

d. Methods--information about how the student teacher taught or will teach something to pupils.

      e. Language--comments about the language the student teacher
         uses while teaching.

      f. Characteristics of Teaching Behavior--general or specific
         information about how the student teacher behaves
         while teaching.

  2. Cooperating Teacher Teaching Behavior--information about the
     behavior of the cooperating teacher as a teacher of
     children.

  3. College Supervisor Teaching Behavior--comments about the work
     or behavior of the college supervisor as a teacher of
     children.

<u>Student Teachers</u>--general and specific information about student teachers
    as learners and the particular problems they have in connection
    with taking the role of a teacher.

<u>Student Teacher</u>--general comments about the student teacher assigned to
    the participating cooperating teacher.

  1. Personal--information about the student's temperament,
     character, attitudes, abilities, interests, feelings.

  2. Background--personal, professional, and educational experience
     of the student teacher; future plans.

  3. Concerns--comments about the student's concerns in connection
     with the student teacher's role(s).

  4. Learner--information about what the student has learned,
     is learning, needs to learn, realize, or observe in
     connection with teaching.

<u>Children</u>--general or specific information about a child or group of
    children taught by any teacher in an elementary school.

<u>Curriculum</u>--talk about what is taught to pupils in an elementary school.

<u>Materials</u>--comments about materials used by teachers and/or pupils.

<u>School-Community Situation</u>--information on organizational structure and
    administrative policies, supervision, special teachers; social,
    economic, cultural structure of the community; school-community
    relationships.

<u>College Program</u>--organizational structure, administrative and instruc-
    tional policies; available resources.